The Story of Charle

A Novel.

(Volume II)

GW01402730

Mrs. Henry Wood

Alpha Editions

This edition published in 2024

ISBN : 9789362923288

Design and Setting By
Alpha Editions
www.alphaedis.com
Email - info@alphaedis.com

Contents

CHAPTER I.
SUSPICION.

THE church-clock of that small country place, Upper Marshdale, was chiming half-past nine on a dark night, as the local inspector turned out of the police-station and made his way with a fleet step across a piece of waste land and some solitary fields beyond it. His name was Poole, and he was hastening to Marshdale House, as Lord Level's place was called. A mysterious occurrence had taken place there the night before: Lord Level, previously an invalid, had been stabbed in his bed.

The officer rang a loud peal at the outer gate, and a policeman, who had been already sent on, came from the house to answer the summons. He waited when they were both within the gate, knowing that he should be questioned. His superior walked half-way up the avenue, and placed his back against a tree.

"What have you learnt, Jekyl? Any clue to the assassin?"

The policeman dropped his voice to a whisper, as though afraid the very trees might hear. "Speak up," sharply interrupted the inspector. "The air carries no tales."

"The case seems as clear, sir, as any we ever came across; a clear case against Lady Level."

It takes a great deal to astonish a police inspector, but this announcement certainly astonished Mr. Inspector Poole. "Against Lady Level?" he repeated.

"She's the guilty one, sir, I fear. But who'd think it, to see her? Only about twenty or so, and with beauty enough to knock you over, and blue eyes that look you down in their pride. She's dressed out like those high-born ladies do dress, in light silk that glistens as she walks, her neck and arms uncovered. There's a gentleman with her now, some friend of the family, and he won't let us go on with our investigation. He came and stopped it, and said we were acting against Lord Level's wishes."

"But why do you suspect Lady Level?" inquired the inspector.

"Listen, sir. It appears certain that no one got in; the doors and windows were left safe, and were found so; hadn't been disturbed at all; there has been no robbery, or anything of that sort, and no suspicion attaches to any of the servants so far as I see. Then there are the facts themselves. The servants were aroused in the middle of the night by Lord Level's bell ringing violently, and my lady screaming. When they got to his room, there he lay, fainted dead off, stabbed in two places, and she pretty near fainting too, and dropped down in a chair in her silk dressing-gown———"

"I am acquainted with the facts so far, Jekyl."

"Well, sir. Not a sign or symptom was there of anybody else being about, or of anybody's having been about. Her ladyship's version is, that she was woke up by Lord Level calling to her, and she found him stabbed and bleeding. That is all she will confess to."

"And he?"

"He says nothing, I hear, except that he will not have the police called in. He did not even want to have a doctor. But his lordship is off his head with fever, and may not know what he is saying."

"How does Lady Level account for the knife being found in her room?"

"There it is," cried the man. "Whenever these people, let them be high or low, do an evil deed, they are certain to commit some act of folly which allows suspicion to creep in. They over-do it, or they under-do it. If anyone else had done it and carried the weapon to her ladyship's room, she must have seen who it was, and would surely have denounced him. And why did *she* put it there of all places? There's a fatality on them, I say, sir, and they can't escape it."

"But her motive for attacking him?"

"They were on bad terms, it seems. The servants heard them quarrelling violently earlier in the evening."

"Did the servants tell you this, to confirm their suspicions against her?"

"They don't suspect her, sir," replied Jekyl. "I and Cliff have drawn our own deductions by what they have said, and by personal observation."

The inspector mused. He was a kindly-disposed man, possessed his share of common sense, and did not feel so sure about the matter as his subordinate. "It appears scarcely credible that a young woman like Lady Level, hardly six months married, should attempt her husband's life, Jekyl. Where are these servants?"

"In the kitchen, sir. This way. There's no establishment to speak of. When my lord was detained here through damage to his knee, my lady followed him down—against his will, it's whispered—and brought only her maid and a man-servant."

"I think you have been listening to a good deal of gossip," remarked Inspector Poole, as he moved on to the house.

Meanwhile Lady Level, in deep agitation, stood at the window which she had had thrown up for air, while she made the confession to Mr. Ravensworth that she had been a witness to the attack on her husband. This she had denied before; and it might never have been wrung from her, but that she overheard the two policemen, already in the house, whispering their suspicions against her.

She was shocked, indignant, terrified. She leaned for support on the window-frame, panting for breath in the cold night air.

"Arnold, am I to bear this?"

He stood with folded arms. He felt for her deeply: were she connected with him by near ties of blood, he could not have been more anxious to protect her; but a strong doubt that she *might* be guilty was working within him. He supposed she must have received some great provocation from Lord Level.

"How cruel they are to entertain such a suspicion! If they—if they—— Oh, Arnold, they never will arrest me!—they never will publicly accuse me!" she uttered, as a new possibility occurred to her.

"Blanche, listen," he rejoined, talking to her as he had talked when she was a child. "All that can be done for you, I will do; but I cannot work in this uncertainty. Tell me the truth; be it good or be it ill, I will stand by you; but, if I am to be of service to you, I must know it. Was it you who struck Lord Level?"

"No. Have I not just told you so?"

"What you told me I do not understand. You say you saw it done——"

"Then I did not see it done," she petulantly interrupted; and no more questions would she answer.

"Let me take you back to the fire," said Mr. Ravensworth, as he shut down the window. "You are trembling with cold."

"Not with cold," was her reply.

Stirring the fire into a blaze, he drew the easy-chair near it for her. He then stood by, saying nothing.

"Suppose they should openly accuse me?" she began, after a silence. "Would they arrest me?"

"Blanche," he retorted, in sharp, ringing, imperative accents, "are you guilty? Tell me, one way or the other, that I may know what to be at."

Lady Level rose and confronted him, her blue eyes wearing their most haughty expression. "You have known me for many years, known me well; how then can you repeat that question? *I* guilty of attacking Lord Level!"

"I would rather believe myself—I could as soon believe my own wife guilty of such a thing; but why have you equivocated with me? You have not told me the truth, as to what passed that night."

"My husband charged me not to tell anyone."

"Five minutes ago you told me yourself that you saw it done; now you say you did not see it. What am I to think?"

"In saying I saw it done, I spoke hastily; what I ought to have said was, that I saw who did it. And then, to-day, Lord Level insisted that I had been dreaming," she abstractedly continued. "Arnold, do you believe that we can see visions or dream dreams that afterwards wear the semblance of realities?"

"I wish you would not speak in riddles. The time is going on; those men of the law may come in and accuse you, and what defence am I to make for you? You know that you may trust me. What you say shall never pass my lips."

Lady Level deliberated. "I will trust you," she said at length: "there seems to be no help for it. I went to rest last night angry with Lord Level, for we had spoken irritating words to each other. I lay awake, I dare say for an hour, indulging bitter thoughts, and then I dropped asleep. Suddenly something woke me; I cannot tell you what it was: whether it was any noise, or whether it was the opening of the door, which I had closed, between my room and Lord Level's. All I know is, that door was wide open, and someone stood in the doorway with a lighted candle. It was a strange-looking object, and seemed to be dressed in flannel—either a long flannel shirt or a flannel gown. In the confusion of the moment I believed it must be Lord Level, and I was struck with amazement, for Lord Level is not able to get out of bed without assistance, from the injury to his knee, and I thought how long his hair was, and how dark it had grown—that was, you know, when I was between sleeping and waking. Then I saw that it had large, flashing black eyes, so it could not be Lord Level. It crossed the room——"

"Blanche," he interrupted, "you speak just as if you were describing a vision. It——"

"That is what Lord Level now says it was. Let me go on. It crossed the room as far as the dressing-table. I started up in bed then, and the wild eyes turned upon me, and at the same moment Lord Level called out from his own bed, apparently in agitation or pain. The figure dropped something, turned round, and darted back again through the open door to the other chamber. I saw the candle fall from its hand to the floor, and the place was in darkness, except for the little light that came from Lord Level's night-lamp. Terror overwhelmed me, and I cried out, and then my husband called to me by name. I ran to his room, flinging on my warm silk dressing-gown as I went, and there I found him hurt in some way, for he was bleeding from the arm and from the side. Arnold, as I live, as I breathe, that is the whole truth," she concluded with emotion.

"Did you again see the figure? Was it in Lord Level's room?"

"It was not there. I saw no trace of it. I remember I picked up the candlestick, for it was right in my path, and I screamed when I saw the blood upon my husband. He caught me to him by the other arm, as I have told you, telling me not to be frightened, that he would protect me; and I saw how white he looked, and that his brow was damp. Presently I asked him who and what it was; and the question seemed to excite him. 'Say nothing of what you have seen,' he cried; 'I charge you, *nothing*.' I don't quite know what I replied; it was to the effect that the household must be aroused, and the figure searched for. 'Blanche, you are my wife,' he said solemnly; 'my interests are yours; I charge you, by your duty and obedience to me, that you say nothing. Bury this in silence, as you value your life and mine.' Then he fainted and his hold relaxed, and I screamed out and the servants came. Had my life depended upon it I could not have helped screaming. What the figure had dropped in my room proved to be the knife."

"This is a very strange account!" exclaimed Mr. Ravensworth.

"It is so strange that I lose myself at times, wondering whether I was dreaming or awake. But it was true; it was true; though I could not proclaim it in defiance of my husband."

"Do you think the figure, as you call it, could have been one of the servants in disguise?"

"I am certain it was not. Not one of them has that dark Italian face."

"Italian face!" echoed Mr. Ravensworth. "Why do you call it an Italian face?"

Lady Level bent her head. "The thought somehow struck me," she answered, after a pause. "Not at the time, but since. I fancied it not unlike the Italian faces that one sees in pictures."

"Was it a man or a woman?"

"I do not know. At the time I took it to be a man, quite young. But since, recalling the appearance—well, it seems to me that it is impossible to decide which it was."

"And you saw no signs of this mysterious figure afterwards?"

"None whatever. There were no traces, I tell you, of its having been there, except the injury to Lord Level, the knife, and the fallen candlestick. The candlestick may have been left in Lord Level's room the previous night, for it is precisely like those used in the household, so that the figure may have lighted it from the night-lamp."

Mr. Ravensworth could not make much of all this. It puzzled him. "The curious thing is," he said aloud, "where could the figure have come from?"

"The curious thing is, that Lord Level wants to persuade me now that this was only a dream of the imagination."

"That his wounds are?"

"Not his wounds, of course—or the knife, but a great deal of what I told him. He ridicules the bare idea of its being a 'strange figure,' 'strangely dressed.' He says he caught a full view of the man who attacked him; that he should know him again; that he was dressed in a sort of soft light fustian, and was no more wild-looking than I am, except such wildness as arose from his state of inebriation, and he suspects he was a poacher who must have got in through one of the windows."

Mr. Ravensworth pondered over the tale: and he could not help deeming it a most improbable one. But that traces of some mysterious presence had been left behind, he would have regarded it as her husband appeared partially to regard it—a midnight freak of Lady Level's imagination. "Yet the wounds are realities," said Mr. Ravensworth, speaking aloud, in answer to his own thoughts.

"Arnold, it is all a reality," she said impressively. "There are moments, I say, when I am almost tempted to question it, but in my sober reason I know it to have been true; and while I ask myself, 'Was it a dream?' I hold a perfect, positive conviction that it was only too terrible a reality."

"You have spoken once or twice of its wild appearance. Did it look like a madman?"

"I never saw a madman, that I know of. This creature looked wild enough to be mad. There was one thing I thought curious in connection with finding the knife," proceeded Lady Level. "Timms, who picked it up, while Sanders had gone down for some hot water, brought it into Lord Level's room, calling out that she had found the weapon. 'Why, that's Mr. Drewitt's knife!' exclaimed the housemaid, Deborah, as soon as she saw it; and the steward, who had only just reached the room, asked her how she could make the assertion. 'It is yours, sir,' said Deborah; 'it's your new knife; I have seen it on your table, and should know it anywhere.' 'Deborah, if you repeat that again, I'll have you punished,' sharply called out the housekeeper, without, you understand, turning from Lord Level, to whom she was attending, to ascertain whether it was or was not the knife. Now, Arnold," added Lady Level, "ill and terrified as I felt at the moment, a conviction came across me that it was Mr. Drewitt's knife, but that he and Mrs. Edwards were purposely denying it."

"It is impossible to suspect them of attacking, or conniving at the attack on Lord Level."

"They attack Lord Level! They would rather attack the whole world combined, than that a hair of his head should suffer. They are fondly, devotedly attached to him. And Deborah, it appears, has been convinced out of her assertion. Hark! who is that?"

Mr. Ravensworth opened the door to reconnoitre. The inspector was prowling about the house and passages, exploring the outlets and inlets, followed by his two men, who had done the same before him.

"I thought you had forbidden the men to search," cried Lady Level. "Why are they disobeying you?"

"Their chief is here now, and of course his orders go before mine. Besides, after what you have told me, I consider there ought to be a thorough search," added Mr. Ravensworth.

"In opposition to Lord Level?"

"I think that Lord Level has not taken a sufficiently serious view of the case. The only solution I can come to is, that some escaped madman got into the house before it was closed for the night, and concealed himself in it. If so, he may be in it now."

"Now! In it now!" she exclaimed, turning pale.

"Upon my word, I think it may be so. The doors and windows were all found safely fastened, you see. Therefore he could not escape during the night. And since the doors were opened this morning, the household, I take it, has been so constantly on the alert, that it might be an extremely difficult matter for him to get away unseen. If he, this madman, did enter yesterday evening, he must have found some place of concealment and hidden himself in it for hours, since it was not until one o'clock that he made the attack on Lord Level."

"Oh, Arnold, that is all too improbable," she rejoined doubtingly. "A madman could not plan and do all that."

"Madmen are more cunning than sane ones, sometimes."

"But I—I think it was a woman," said Lady Level, lowering her voice and her eyes.

Mr. Ravensworth looked at her. And for the first time, a feeling flashed into his mind that Lady Level had some suspicion which she would not speak of.

"Blanche," he said sharply, "do you know who it was? Tell me, if you do."

"I do not," she answered emphatically. "I may imagine this and imagine that, but I do not know anything."

"You were speaking, then, from imagination?"

"Y—es. In a case of mystery, such as this, imagination runs riot, and you can't prevent its doing so."

Again there was something about Lady Level that struck Mr. Ravensworth as being not honestly true. Before more could be said, steps were heard approaching the room; and Lady Level, afraid to meet the police, made her escape from it.

Running swiftly upstairs, she was passing Lord Level's door to enter her own, when she heard his voice, speaking collectedly, and peeped in. He saw her, and held out his hand. He appeared now quite rational, though his fine gray eyes were glistening and his fair face was flushed. Mrs. Edwards was standing by the bedside, and it was to her he had been talking.

Blanche advanced timidly. "Are you feeling better?" she softly asked.

"Oh, much better; nearly well: but for my knee I should be up and about," he answered, as he drew her towards him. "Mrs. Edwards, will you close the door? I wish to speak with my wife."

Mrs. Edwards, with a warning glance at her lady, which seemed to say, "He is not fit for it"—at least Blanche so interpreted it—went out and shut the door. Lord Level drew her closer to his side. He was lying propped up by a mound of pillows, almost sitting up in bed, and kept her standing there.

"Blanche," he began in very quiet tones, "I hear the police are in the house."

"Yes," she was obliged to answer, quite taken aback and feeling very much vexed that he had been told, as it was likely to excite him.

"Who sent for them? You?"

"Oh no."

"Then it was your friend; that fellow Ravensworth. I thought as much."

"But indeed it was not," she eagerly answered, shrinking from her husband's scornful tones. "When the two policemen came in—and we do not know who it was sent them—Mr. Ravensworth went to them by my desire to stop the search. I told him that you objected to it."

"Objected to it! I forbade it," haughtily rejoined Lord Level. "And if—if——"

"Oh, pray, Archibald, do not excite yourself; do not, do not!" she interrupted, frightened and anxious. "You know you will become worse again if you do."

"Will you go and end it in my name? End it, and send them away from the house."

"Yes, if you tell me to do so; if you insist upon it," she answered. "But I am afraid."

"Why are you afraid?"

Lady Level bent her head until it was on a level with his. "For this, Archibald," she whispered: "that they might question me—and I should be obliged to answer them."

Lord Level gently drew her cool cheek nearer, that it might rest against his fevered one, and remained silent, apparently pondering the question.

"After I told you all that I saw that night, you bade me be silent," she resumed. "Well, I fear the police might draw it from me if they questioned me."

"But you must not allow them to draw it from you."

"Oh, but perhaps I could not help it," she sighed. "You know what the police are—how they question and cross-question people."

"Blanche, I reminded you last night that you were my wife, and you owed me implicit obedience in all great things."

"Yes, and I am trying to obey you; I am indeed, Archibald," she protested, almost torn by conflicting emotions; for, in spite of her doubts and suspicions, and (as she put it to herself) her "wrongs," she loved her husband yet.

"Well, my dear, you must be brave for my sake; ay, and for your own. Listen, Blanche: you will tell the police *nothing*; and they *must not search the house*. I don't care to see them myself to forbid it; I don't want to see them.

For one thing, I am hardly strong enough to support the excitement it would cause me. But——"

"Will you tell me something, Archibald?" she whispered. "Is the—the—person—that attacked you in the house now?"

Lord Level looked surprised. "In this house? Why, how could it be? Certainly not."

"Was it—was it a woman?" she breathed, her voice low and tremulous.

He turned angry. "How can you be so silly, Blanche? A woman! Oh yes," changing to sarcasm, "of course it was a woman. It was you, perhaps."

"That is what they are saying, Archibald."

"*What* are they saying?" he returned, in dangerous excitement—if Blanche had only noticed the signs. For all this was agitating him.

"Why, that," she answered, bursting into tears. "The police are saying so. They are saying that it was I who stabbed you."

Lord Level cried out as a man in agony. And, with that, delirium came on again.

CHAPTER II.
NOT LIFTED.

MY Lady Level sat at the open window of her husband's sitting-room, in the dark, her hot face lifted to the cool night air. Only a moment ago Lord Level had been calling out in his delirium, and Mrs. Edwards was putting cool appliances to his head, and damp, hot bricks to his feet. And Blanche knew that it was she who, by her indiscreet remarks and questioning, had brought on the crisis. She had not meant to harm or excite him; but she had done it; and she was very contrite.

It was now between ten and eleven o'clock. She did not intend to go to bed that night; and she had already slipped off her evening dress, and put on a morning one of soft gray cashmere. With his lordship in a fresh attack of fever, and the police about, the household did not think of going to rest.

Blanche Level sat in a miserable reverie, her lovely face pressed upon her slender hand, the tears standing in her blue eyes. She was suspecting her husband of all kinds of unorthodox things—this has been said before. Not the least disloyal of them being that an individual named Nina, who wore long gold earrings to enhance her charms, was concealed in that east wing, which might almost be called a separate house, and which owned a separate entrance.

And a conviction lay upon Lady Level—caught up since, not at the time— that it was this Nina who had attacked Lord Level. She could not drive away the impression.

Naturally she was bitterly resentful. Not at the attack, but at all the rest of it. She had said nothing yet to her husband, and she did not know whether she ever should say it; for even to speak upon such a topic reflected on herself a shame that stung her. *Of course* he forbade the search lest this visitor should be discovered, reasoned she; that is, he told her to forbid it: but ought she to obey him? Lady Level, cowering there in the darkness, would have served as a perfect exemplification of a small portion of Collins's "Ode to the Passions."

'Thy numbers, Jealousy, to naught were fixed,
Sad proof of thy distressful state;
Of differing themes the veering song was mixed,
And now it courted love, now raving, called on hate.'

Thus was it here. One moment she felt that she could—and should—put Lord Level away from her for his falsity, his treachery; the next she was conscious that life without him would be one long and bitter penance, for she had learned to love him with her whole heart and soul.

And until that miserable sojourn at Pisa, she had deemed that he returned her love, truly and passionately. Fie on the deceitful wiles of man!

A stir in the passage without. Was there any change in Lord Level, for better or for worse? Despite her resentment, she was anxious, and she opened the door. Mrs. Edwards had come out from the opposite chamber, a basin in hand.

"My lady, he is calmer," whispered the housekeeper, answering the unspoken question which she read in her eyes. "If he could only be kept so, if he had nothing to disturb him, he would soon be well again. It is a most unlucky thing that these police should have come here, where they are not wanted. That of itself must bring excitement to his lordship."

"It is unlucky that these tales should have been carried to him," haughtily reproved the young lady. "I cannot think who does it, or why."

"Nay, my lady, but when his lordship questions of this and that, he must be answered."

Closing the door of the sick-chamber very quietly, Mrs. Edwards passed down the stairs. At the same moment, covert steps were heard ascending them. Lady Level caught a glimpse of Mr. Inspector Poole's head, and stole back out of sight.

Meanwhile Mr. Ravensworth had been trying to gain a little explanation from that official. "Do you know," he said to him, "that you are here against Lord Level's wishes, and in direct opposition to his orders?"

"No, I do not," replied the inspector. "I did not understand it in that light. I certainly was told that his lordship had said he would not have the case officially inquired into, but I understood that he was lightheaded when he spoke, not at all conscious of what he was saying."

"From whom, then, did you receive your instructions, Mr. Poole?"

"From Dr. Macferraty," was the ready answer. "He called in at the station this evening."

"Ah!" cried Arnold Ravensworth.

"It would be a grave mistake, he said, if so monstrous a thing—they were the doctors own words—should be left uninvestigated, because his lordship was off his head," added the inspector. "May I ask, sir, if you entertain any suspicion—in any quarter?"

"Not any," decisively replied Mr. Ravensworth. "The whole thing is to me most mysterious."

The speakers looked at one another. Mr. Poole was deliberating whether he should give a hint of what Jekyl had said about Lady Level. But he was saved the trouble.

"I understand, through overhearing a word or two, that your men have been wondering whether the culprit could have been Lady Level," spoke Mr. Ravensworth in low tones. "The very idea is monstrous: you have but now used the right word. *Believe me*, she is innocent as a child. But she is most terribly frightened."

"Well, I thought it very unlikely," admitted the inspector.

"But it seems," slowly continued Mr. Ravensworth, weighing well his words, "that she caught sight at the time, or thought she caught sight, of a figure curiously attired in white flannel, who dropped, or flung, the knife down in her chamber. Lord Level says it was not white flannel, but light fustian, such as a countryman might wear. According to that, he must also have seen the individual. The difficulty, however, is, to know whether his lordship is speaking in his senses or out of them."

"Someone must have got in, then, after all; in spite of the doors being found as they were left."

"I think so. I cannot see any other loophole for suspicion to fall back upon. Concealed himself in the house probably beforehand. And, for all we know, may be concealed in it still. I gathered an impression while Lady Level was talking to me that it might really be some escaped madman. All the same, Lord Level persists in forbidding the matter to be investigated."

Keen and practical, the officer revolved what he heard. The story was a curious one altogether, and as yet he did not see his way in it.

"I think, sir," he said with deliberation, "that I shall take the affair into my hands, and act, in the uncertain state of his lordship's mind, upon my own responsibility. First of all, we will just go through the house."

Mr. Ravensworth went with him: they two together. After a thorough search, nothing wrong could they find or discover. The servants and the two policemen remained below; Mrs. Edwards was in close attendance upon his lordship; and the steward, who appeared most exceedingly to resent the presence of these police in the house, had shut himself into his rooms.

In the course of time, the inspector and Mr. Ravensworth approached these rooms. Passing Lord Level's chamber with soft footsteps, they traversed the passages beyond it, until they found themselves stopped by a door, which was fastened.

Mr. Poole shook it. "It must lead to some of the remote rooms," he observed, "and they are uninhabited. Just the spot for an assassin to conceal himself in—or to try to do so."

"I think these may be the steward's apartments," spoke Arnold Ravensworth doubtingly. "I remember Lady Level said they were only divided from his lordship's chamber by a passage or two."

Whose ever rooms they were, no one came to the door in answer to the summons, and the inspector knocked again.

This time it brought forth Mr. Drewitt. They heard him draw a chain, and then he opened the door a few inches, as far as the chain permitted him.

"Will you let us in, Mr. Drewitt? I must search these rooms."

"Search for what?" asked the old man. "It's you, is it, Poole! I cannot have my rooms searched. This morning, after the alarm, I went over them, to be quite sure, and that's sufficient."

"Allow me to search for myself," returned the officer.

"No, sir," answered the steward, with dignity. "No one shall come in to search these rooms in opposition to the wish of my lord. His orders to me were that the affair should be allowed to drop, and I for one will not disobey him, or give help to those who would. His lordship believed that whoever it might be that attacked him came in and went out again. The country might be hunted over, he said, but not his house."

"I must enter here," was all the answer reiterated by the officer.

"It shall be over my body, then," returned the steward, with emotion. "My lord forbade a search, and you have no right whatever to proceed with it."

"My good man, I am a police inspector."

"You may be inspector-general for all I care," retorted the old gentleman, "but you don't come in here. Get my lord's authority first, and then you will be welcome. As to reminding me who you are, Mr. Poole, you must know that to be superfluous. And I beg *your* pardon, sir," he added, addressing Mr. Ravensworth, "but I would inquire what authority you hold from my lord, that you, a stranger, should set at naught his expressed wishes?"

The door was shut and bolted in their faces, and the inspector leaned against the wall in thought. "Did you notice his agitation?" he whispered to Mr. Ravensworth. "There's more in this than meets the eye."

It certainly wore that appearance. However, for the present they were foiled, and the steward remained master of the position. To attempt to enter those rooms by force would create noise and commotion in the house that might be disastrous to the health of Lord Level.

"There's *something* in those rooms that has to be concealed," spoke the astute inspector. "If it be the man who attacked Lord Level——"

"But the steward, devoted as he is to his master, would not harbour *him*," impulsively interrupted Arnold Ravensworth.

"True. Unless—unless, mind you, there exists some cause, which we cannot even guess at, for his lordship's shielding him," said the inspector. "I must say I should like to get into the rooms."

"There is no other way of doing it; no other entrance."

"I don't know that, sir. Unless I am mistaken, these rooms communicate direct with the East Wing. By getting into that, we might find an unsuspected entrance."

He made his way downstairs in silence, musing as he went. At the foot of the staircase he encountered Deborah.

"Which are the passages in this lower part of the house that lead to the East Wing?" he inquired.

"Not any of them, sir," answered Deborah promptly. "At least, not any that are ever opened. At the end of the stone passage there's a heavy door, barred and bolted, that leads to other passages, I believe, and to other heavy bolted doors, and they lead into the East Wing. That's what I have heard say. The only entrance in use is the one through Mr. Drewitt's rooms."

Opposition seemed only to strengthen the will of Mr. Inspector Poole. "Into the rooms I mean to make my way," he said to Mr. Ravensworth, as he retraced his steps up the staircase. "Could you not," he hastily added, "get Lady Level to bring her authority to bear upon old Drewitt?"

It was the appearance of Lady Level that probably induced the thought. She, looking pale, haggard and uneasy, was peeping down at them, and did not escape in time.

Arnold Ravensworth somewhat hesitatingly acceded. They wished to speak to Mr. Drewitt—he put it to her in that way—but he had bolted himself into his rooms; would she use her authority and bid him admit them?

She complied at once, unsuspiciously. Of all parts of the house, that occupied by the steward must be most free from concealment. And she went with them to the barred-up door.

The steward did not presume to dispute Lady Level's mandate, which she gave somewhat imperiously. She entered with them. They found themselves in the old gentleman's sitting-room, and he placed chairs for them. "We have not come to sit down," said Mr. Poole; and he passed into the other rooms in rapid succession: the two bed-chambers and the unoccupied room that had nothing in it but a few trunks. A very cursory inspection convinced him that no person was being harboured there.

"Why could you not have admitted us just now, Mr. Drewitt?" he asked.

"Because you brought not the authority of either my lord or my lady," answered the faithful old retainer.

The inspector strode to the end of the passage and stood before the oaken door already spoken of, examining its heavy fastenings. The others had followed him.

"This must be the door communicating between the house and the East Wing," he remarked. "Will you open it, Mr. Drewitt?"

"No, sir, I will not."

"But we must have it opened," interposed Arnold Ravensworth. "The fact is, we have some reason to fear the midnight assassin may yet be hiding himself on the premises. He does not appear to be in the house, so he may be in the East Wing—and we mean to search it."

"Are you an enemy of my lord's?" returned the old man, greatly agitated.

"Certainly not. I would rather be his friend. I have been the friend, if I may so express it, of Lady Level since she was a child, and I must see that she is protected, her husband being for the time laid aside."

"My lady," called out the old man, visibly trembling, "I appeal to you, as my lord's second self, to forbid these gentlemen from attempting to enter the East Wing."

"Be firm, Blanche," whispered Mr. Ravensworth, as she came forward. "We must search the East Wing, and it is for your sake."

She turned to the steward. "I am sure that they are acting for the best. Open the door."

For one moment the old man hesitated, and then wrung his hands. "That I should be forced to disobey the wife of my lord! My lady, I crave your pardon, but I will not open these rooms unless I have the express authority of his lordship to do so."

"But I wish it done, Mr. Drewitt," she said, blushing hotly.

Police inspectors have generally the means of carrying out their own will. Mr. Poole, after critically regarding the fastenings, produced one or two small instruments from his pockets and a bunch of keys. As he was putting one of the keys into the lock for the purpose of trying whether it would fit it, a curious revulsion came over Lady Level. Possibly the piteous, beseeching countenance of the steward induced it. "He *is* my husband, after all," she whispered to her own heart.

"Stop!" she said aloud, pushing the key downwards. "I may not have the right to sanction this in opposition to the wish of Lord Level. He has forbidden any search to be made, and I must do the same."

There was a moment's silence. The inspector gazed at her.

"When his lordship shall be sufficiently recovered to see you, sir, you can take instructions from him if he sees well to give them," she added to the officer civilly. "Until then, I must act for him, and I forbid——"

"Highty-tighty, and what's the matter here?" broke in a hearty voice behind them, at which they all turned in surprise. Making his way along the passage was a portly, but rather short man of sixty years, with an intellectual brow and benevolent countenance, a red face and a bald head. The change in Mr. Drewitt's look was remarkable; its piteousness had changed to radiance.

The new-comer shook hands with him. Then he turned and affably shook hands with the inspector, speaking gaily. "You look as if you had the business of all the world on your shoulders, Poole."

"Have you seen my lord, Mr. Hill?" asked the steward.

"I got back home to-night and came on here at once, hearing of the hubbub you are in, and I have seen my lord for a few minutes. And this is my lady—and a very charming lady I am sure she is," he added, bowing to Lady Level with an irresistible smile. "Will she shake hands with the old man who has been doctor-in-ordinary to her lord's family for ages and ages?"

Blanche put her hand into his. She, as she was wont sometimes to tell him in days to come, fell in love with him at once.

"What a blessing that you are back again!" murmured the good old steward.

"Ay," assented Mr. Hill, perhaps purposely misinterpreting the remark: "we will have Lord Level up and about in no time now.—Mr. Poole, I want a private word with you."

The doctor drew him into the steward's sitting-room, and closed the door. The conference did not last more than a minute or two, but it was very effectual. For when Mr. Inspector Poole came forth, he announced his decision of withdrawing all search at present. To be resumed if necessary, he added, when his lordship should have recovered sufficiently to give his own orders.

The only one who did not appear to be altogether satisfied with this summary check was Arnold Ravensworth. He did not understand it. Upon some remark being made as to Lady Level's safety from any attack by the midnight villain, Mr. Hill at once told her *he* would guarantee that. And though he spoke with a laugh, as if making light of the matter, there was an assurance in his eye and tone that she might implicitly trust to.

"Then—as it seems I cannot be of any further use to you to-night, and as I may just catch the midnight up-train, I will wish you good-bye, Lady Level," said Mr. Ravensworth. "I am easy about you, now Mr. Hill is here. But be sure to write for me if you think I can be of service to you or to Lord Level."

"I will, I will," she answered. "Thank you, Arnold, for coming."

Marshdale House returned to its usual monotony, and a day or two went on. Nothing more was seen or heard of the unknown individual who had so disturbed its peace; the very mention of it was avoided. Nevertheless, Blanche, turning matters over in her mind, could only look at it and at that detestable East Wing with an increased sense of mystery. "But for knowing that someone was there who might not be disclosed to the honest light of day, why should he have forbidden the search?" ran the argument that she was for ever holding with herself; and she steeled her heart yet more against her husband.

On this, the second afternoon after the commotion, she was sitting reading a newspaper in the garden, where the sun was shining hotly, when Mr. Hill, who had been up with Lord Level, appeared.

"Well," said the doctor cheerily, halting before her, "he is a great deal better, and the knee's ever so much stronger. I shall have him up to-morrow. And in a couple of days after that he may venture to travel to town, as he is so anxious to get there."

"Your treatment seems to agree with him better than Dr. Macferraty's did," she answered.

"Ay: I know his constitution, you see. Good-day, Lady Level. I shall be in again to-night."

Soon after the doctor went out, there was heard a shrill whistle at the gate, together with a kicking about of gravel by a pair of rough boots. Lady Level looked up, and saw the boy from the station bringing in a parcel.

"Well, Sam," said she, as the lad approached. "What have you come for?"

"They sent me on with this here parcel—and precious heavy he is for his size," replied Sam Doughty, as without ceremony he tumbled the parcel on to the bench by Lady Level's side. It was addressed to her, and she knew that it contained some books which Mr. Ravensworth had promised to send down. "Come down by the mid-day train," curtly added the boy for her information.

"Do you get paid for delivering parcels, Sam?"

"*Me* get paid!" returned the youth, with intense aggravation; "no such luck. Unless," added he, a happy thought striking him, "anybody likes to give me something for myself—knowing how weighty they be, and what a lug it is for one's arms."

"This parcel is not at all heavy," said Lady Level.

"I'm sure he is, then, for his size. You should lift, though, what I have to drag along sometimes. Why, yesterday that ever was, I brought a parcel as big as a house to the next door; one that come from Lunnon by the mid-day train just as this'n did; and Mother Snow she never gave me nothing but a jam tart, no bigger nor the round o' your hand. She were taking a tray on 'em out o' the oven."

"Jam tarts for *her* delectation!" was the thought that flashed through Lady Level's mind. "Who was the parcel for, Sam?" she asked aloud.

"'Twere directed to Mrs. Snow."

"Oh. Not to that lady who is staying there?"

"What lady be that?" questioned Sam.

"The one you told me about. The lady with the long gold earrings."

Sam's stolid countenance assumed a look of doubt, as if he did not altogether understand. His eyes grew wider.

"*That* un! Her bain't there now, her bain't. Her didn't stop. Her went right away again the next day after she come."

"*Did* she?" exclaimed Lady Level, taken by surprise. "Are you sure?"

"Be I sure as that's a newspaper in your hand?" retorted Sam. "In course I be sure. The fly were ordered down here for her the next morning, and she come on to the station in it, Mr. Snow a sitting outside."

"She went back to London, then!"

"She went just t'other way," contradicted the boy. "Right on by the down-train. Dover her ticket were took for."

Lady Level fell into a passing reverie. All the conjectures she had been indulging in lately—whither had they flown? At that moment Mrs. Edwards, having seen the boy from the house, came out to ask what he wanted. Sam put on his best behaviour instantly. The respect he failed to show to the young lady was in full force before Mrs. Edwards.

"I come to bring this here parcel, please, ma'am, for Lady Level," said he, touching his old cap.

"Oh, very well," said Mrs. Edwards. "I'll carry it indoors, my lady," she added, taking it up. "You need not wait, Sam."

Lady Level slipped a sixpence into his ready hand, and he went off contented. Mrs. Edwards carried away the parcel.

Presently Lady Level followed, her mind busy as she went upstairs. She was taking some contrition to herself. What if—if it was all, or a great deal of it, only her imagination—that her husband was not the disloyal man she had deemed him?

His chamber door was closed; she passed it and went into her own. Then she opened the door separating the rooms and peeped in. He was lying upon the bed, partly dressed, and wrapped in a warm dressing-gown; his face was turned to the pillow, and he was apparently asleep.

She stole up and stood looking at him. Not a trace of fever lingered in his face now; his fine features looked wan and delicate. Her love for him was making itself heard just then. Cautiously she stooped to imprint a soft, silent kiss upon his cheek; and then another.

She would have lifted her face then, and found she could not do so. His arm was round her in a trice, holding it there; his beautiful gray eyes had opened and were fixed on hers.

"So you care for me a little bit yet, Blanche," he fondly whispered. "Better this than calling me hard names."

She burst into tears. "I should care for you always, Archibald, if—if—I were sure you cared for me."

"You may be very sure of *that*," he emphatically answered. "Let there be peace between us, at any rate, my dear wife. The clouds will pass away in time."

On the Monday morning following, Lord and Lady Level departed for London. The peace, patched up between them, being honestly genuine and hopeful on his lordship's part, but doubtful on that of my lady.

Still nothing had been said or done to lift the mystery which hung about Marshdale.

CHAPTER III.
ONE NIGHT IN ESSEX STREET.

WE go on now to the following year: and I, Charles Strange, take up the narrative again.

It has been said that the two rooms on the ground-floor of our house in Essex Street were chiefly given over to the clerks. I had a desk in the front office; the same desk that I had occupied as a boy; and I frequently sat at it now. Mr. Lennard's desk stood opposite to mine. On the first floor the large front room was furnished as a sitting-room. It was called Mr. Brightman's room, and there he received his clients. The back room was called my room; but Mr. Brightman had a desk in it, and I had another. His desk stood in the middle of the room before the hearthrug; mine was under the window.

One fine Saturday afternoon in February, when it was getting near five o'clock, I was writing busily at my desk in this latter room, when Mr. Brightman came in.

"Rather dark for you, is it not, Charles?" he remarked, as he stirred the fire and sat down in his arm-chair beside it.

"Yes, sir; but I have almost finished."

"What are you going to do with yourself to-morrow?" he presently asked, when I was putting up my parchments.

"Nothing in particular, sir." I could not help sometimes retaining my old way of addressing him, as from clerk to master. "Last Sunday I was with my uncle Stillingfar."

"Then you may as well come down to Clapham and dine with me. Mrs. Brightman is away for a day or two, and I shall be alone. Come in time for service."

I promised, and drew a chair to the fire, ready to talk with Mr. Brightman. He liked a little chat with me at times when the day's work was over. It turned now on Lord Level, from whom I had heard that morning. We were not his usual solicitors, but were doing a little matter of business for him. He and Blanche had been abroad since the previous November (when they had come up together from Marshdale), and had now been in Paris for about a month.

"Do they still get on pretty well?" asked Mr. Brightman: for he knew that there had been differences between them.

"Pretty well," I answered, rather hesitatingly.

And, in truth, it was only pretty well, so far as I was able to form a judgment. During this sojourn of theirs in Paris I had spent a few days there with a client, and saw Blanche two or three times. That she was living in a state of haughty resentment against her husband was indisputable. Why or wherefore, I knew not. She dropped a mysterious word to me now and then, of which I could make nothing.

While Mr. Brightman was saying this, a clerk came in, handed a letter to him and retired.

"What a nuisance!" cried he, as he read it by fire-light. I looked up at the exclamation.

"Sir Edmund Clavering's coming to town this evening, and wants me to be here to see him!" he explained. "I can't go home to dinner now."

"Which train is he coming by?" I asked.

"One that is due at Euston Square at six o'clock," replied Mr. Brightman, referring to the letter. "I wanted to be home early this evening."

"You are not obliged to wait, sir," I said. I wished to my heart later—oh, how I wished it!—that he had not waited!

"I suppose I must, Charles. He is a good client, and easily takes offence. Recollect that breeze we had with him three or four months ago."

The clocks struck five as he spoke, and we heard the clerks leaving as usual. I have already stated that no difference was made in the working hours on Saturdays in those days. Afterwards, Mr. Lennard came up to ask whether there was anything more to be done.

"Not now," replied Mr. Brightman. "But I tell you what, Lennard," he added, as a thought seemed to occur to him, "you may as well look in again to-night, about half-past seven or eight, if it won't inconvenience you. Sir Edmund Clavering is coming up; I conclude it is for something special; and I may have instructions to give for Monday morning."

"Very well," replied Lennard. "I will come."

He went out as he spoke; a spare, gentlemanly man, with a fair complexion and thin, careworn face. Edgar Lennard was a man of few words, but attentive and always at his post, a most efficient superintendent of the office and of the clerks in general.

He left and Mr. Brightman rose, saying he would go and get some dinner at the Rainbow. I suggested that he should share my modest steak, adding that Leah could as easily send up enough for two as for one: but he preferred to go out. I rang the bell as I heard him close the frontdoor. Watts answered it, and lighted the gas.

"Tell your wife to prepare my dinner at once," I said to him; "or as soon as possible: Mr. Brightman is coming back to-night. You are going out, are you not?"

"Yes, sir, about that business. Mr. Lennard said I had better go as soon as I had had my tea."

"All right. It will take you two or three hours to get there and back again. See to the fire in the next room; it is to be kept up. And, Watts, tell Leah not to trouble about vegetables to-day: I can't wait for them."

In about twenty minutes Leah and the steak appeared. I could not help looking at her as she placed the tray on the table and settled the dishes. Thin, haggard, untidy, Leah presented a strange contrast to the trim, well-dressed upper servant I had known at White Littleham Rectory. It was Watts who generally waited upon me. When Leah knew beforehand that she would have to wait, she put herself straight. Today she had not known. My proper sitting-room upstairs was not much used in winter. This one was warm and comfortable, with the large fire kept in it all day, so I generally remained in it. I was not troubled with clients after office hours.

"I wonder you go such a figure, Leah!" I could not help saying so.

"It is cleaning-day, Mr. Charles. And I did not know I should have to come up here. Watts has just gone out."

"It is a strange thing to me that you cannot get a woman in to help you. I have said so before."

"Ah, sir, nobody knows where the shoe pinches but he who wears it."

With this remark, unintelligible as apropos to the question, and a deep sigh, Leah withdrew. I had finished dinner, and the tray was taken away before Mr. Brightman returned.

"Now I hope Sir Edmund will be punctual," he cried, as we sat together, talking over a glass of sherry. "It is half-past six: time he was here."

"And there he is!" I exclaimed, as a ring and a knock that shook the house resounded in our ears. After five o'clock the front door was always closed.

Watts being out, we heard Leah answer the door in her charming costume. But clients pay little attention to the attire of laundresses in chambers.

"Good heavens! Can Sir Edmund have taken too much!" uttered Mr. Brightman, halting as he was about to enter the other room to receive him. Loud sounds in a man's voice arose from the passage; singing, laughing, joking with Leah. "Open the door, Charles."

I had already opened it, and saw, not Sir Edmund Clavering, but the young country client, George Coney, the son of a substantial and respectable yeoman in Gloucestershire. He appeared to be in exalted spirits, and had a little exceeded, but was very far from being intoxicated.

"What, is Mr. Brightman here? I only expected to see you," cried he, shaking hands with both. "Look here!" holding out a small canvas bag, and rattling it. "What does that sound like?"

"It sounds like gold," said Mr. Brightman.

"Right, Mr. Brightman; thirty golden sovereigns: and I am as delighted with them as if they were thirty hundred," said he, opening the bag and displaying its contents. "Last week I got swindled out of a horse down at home. Thirty pounds I sold him for, and he and the purchaser disappeared and forgot to pay. My father went on at me, like our old mill clacking; not so much for the loss of the thirty pounds, as at my being done: and all the farmers round about clacked at me, like so many more mills. Pleasant, that, for a fellow, was it not?"

"Very," said Mr. Brightman, while I laughed.

"I did not care to stand it," went on George Coney. "I obtained a bit of a clue, and the day before yesterday I came up to London—and I have met with luck. This afternoon I dropped across the very chap, where I had waited for him since the morning. He was going into a public-house, and another with him, and I pinned them in the room, with a policeman outside, and he pretty soon shelled out the thirty pounds, rather than be taken. That's luck, I hope." He opened the bag as he spoke, and displayed the gold.

"Remarkable luck, to get the money," observed Mr. Brightman.

"I expect they had been in luck themselves," continued young Coney, "for they had more gold with them, and several notes. They were for paying me in notes, but 'No, thank ye,' said I, 'I know good gold when I see it, and I'll take it in that.'"

"I am glad you have been so fortunate," said Mr. Brightman. "When do you return home?"

"I did mean to go to-night, and I called to leave with you this small deed that my father said I might as well bring up with me, as I was coming"— producing a thin folded parchment from his capacious pocketbook. "But I began thinking, as I came along, that I might as well have a bit of a spree now I am here, and go down by Monday night's train," added the young man, tying up the bag again, and slipping it into his pocket. "I shall go to a theatre to-night."

"Not with that bag of gold about you?" said Mr. Brightman.

"Why not?"

"Why not? Because you would have no trace of it left to-morrow morning."

George Coney laughed good-humouredly. "I can take care of myself, sir."

"Perhaps so; but you can't take care of the gold. Come, hand it over to me. Your father will thank me for being determined, and you also, Mr. George, when you have cooled down from the seductions of London."

"I may want to spend some of it," returned George Coney. "Let's see how much I have," cried he, turning the loose money out of his pockets. "Four pounds, seven shillings, and a few halfpence," he concluded, counting it up.

"A great deal too much to squander or lose in one night," remarked Mr. Brightman. "Here," added he, unlocking a deep drawer in his desk, "put your bag in here, and come for it on Monday."

George Coney drew the bag from his pocket, but not without a few remonstrative shakes of the head, and put it in the drawer. Mr. Brightman locked it, and restored the bunch of keys to his pocket.

"You are worse than my father is," cried George Coney, half in jest, half vexed at having yielded. "I wouldn't be as close and stingy for anything."

"In telling this story twenty years hence, Mr. George, you will say, What a simpleton I should have made of myself, if that cautious old lawyer Brightman had not been close and stingy!"

George Coney winked at me and laughed. "Perhaps he's right, after all."

"I know I am," said Mr. Brightman. "Will you take a glass of sherry?"

"Well; no, I think I had better not. I have had almost enough already, and I want to carry clear eyes with me to the play. What time does it begin?"

"About seven, I think; but I am not a theatre-goer myself. Strange can tell you."

"Then I shall be off," said he, shaking hands with us, as only a hearty country yeoman knows how to.

He had scarcely gone when Sir Edmund Clavering's knock was heard. Mr. Brightman went with him into the front room, and I sat reading the *Times*. Leah, by the way, had made herself presentable, and looked tidy enough in a clean white cap and apron.

Sir Edmund did not stay long: he left about seven. I heard Mr. Brightman go back after showing him out, and rake the fire out of the grate—he was always timidly cautious about fire—and then he returned to my room.

"No wonder Sir Edmund wanted to see me," cried he. "There's the deuce of a piece of work down at his place. His cousin wants to dispute the will and to turn him out. They have been serving notices on the tenants not to pay the rent."

"What a curious woman she must be!"

Mr. Brightman smiled slightly, but made no answer.

"He did not stay long, sir."

"No, he is going out to dinner."

As Mr. Brightman spoke, he turned up the gas, drew his chair to the desk and sat down, his back then being towards the fire. "I must look over these letters and copies of notices which Sir Edmund brought with him, and has left with me," he remarked. "I don't care to go home directly."

The next minute he was absorbed in the papers. I put down the *Times*, and rose. "You do not want me, I suppose, Mr. Brightman," I said. "I promised Arthur Lake to go to his chambers for an hour."

"I don't want you, Charles. Mind you are not late in coming down to me to-morrow morning."

So I wished him good-night and departed. Arthur Lake, a full-fledged barrister now of the Middle Temple, rented a couple of rooms in one of the courts. His papers were in one room, his bed in the other. He was a steady fellow, as he always had been, working hard and likely to get on. We passed many of our evenings together over a quiet chat and a cigar, I going round to him, or he coming in to me. He had grown up a little, dandified sort of man, good-humouredly insolent as ever when the fit took him: but sterling at heart.

Lake was sitting at the fire waiting for me, and began to grumble at my being late. I mentioned what had hindered me.

"And I have forgotten my cigar-case!" I exclaimed as I sat down. "I had filled it, all ready, and left it on the table."

"Never mind," said Lake. "I laid in a parcel to-day."

But I did mind, for Lake's "parcels" were never good. He would buy his cigars so dreadfully strong. Nothing pleased him but those full-flavoured Lopez, whilst I liked mild Cabanas: so, generally speaking, I kept to my own. However, I took one, and we sat, talking and smoking. I smoked it out, abominable though it was, and took another; but I couldn't stand a second.

"Lake, I cannot smoke your cigars," I said, flinging it into the fire. "You know I never can. I must run and fetch my own. There goes eight o'clock."

"What's the matter with them?" asked Lake: his usual question.

"Everything; they are bad all over. I shall be back in a trice."

I went the quickest way, through the passages, which brought me into Essex Street, and had my latch-key ready to open the door with as I approached the house. There were three of these latchkeys. I had one; Lennard another, for it sometimes happened that he had to come in before or after business hours; and Leah had possession of the third. But I had no use for mine now, for the door was open. A policeman, standing by the area railings, recognised me, and wished me good-evening.

'Whose carelessness is this?' thought I, advancing to the top of the kitchen stairs and calling to Leah.

It appeared useless to call: no Leah made her appearance. I shut the front door and went upstairs, wondering whether Mr. Brightman had left.

Left! I started back as I entered; for there lay Mr. Brightman on the floor by his desk, as if he had pushed back his chair and fallen from it.

"What is the matter?" I exclaimed, throwing my hat anywhere, and hastening to raise him. But his head and shoulders were a dead weight in my arms, and there was an awful look upon his face, as the gaslight fell upon it. A look, in short, of death, and not of an easy death.

My pulses beat quicker, man though I was, and my heart beat with them. Was I alone in that large house with the dead? I let him fall again and rang the bell violently. I rushed to the door and shouted over the banisters for Leah; and just as I was leaping down for the policeman I had seen outside, or any other help that might be at hand, I heard a latch-key inserted into the lock, and Lennard came in with Dr. Dickenson. I knew him well, for he had attended Miss Methold in the days gone by.

As he hastened to Mr. Brightman, Lennard turned to me, speaking in a whisper:

"Mr. Strange, how did it happen? Was he ill?"

"I know nothing about it, Lennard. I came in a minute ago, and found him lying here. What do you know? Had you been here before?"

"I came, as Mr. Brightman had directed," he replied. "It was a little before eight; and when I got upstairs he was lying there as you see. I tried to rouse him, but could not, and I went off for the doctor."

"Did you leave the front door open?"

"I believe I did, in my flurry and haste. I thought of it as I ran up the street, but would not lose time in going back to shut it."

"He is gone, Mr. Strange," said Dr. Dickenson, advancing towards me, for I and Lennard had stood near the door. "It is a case of sudden death."

I sat down, bewildered. I could not believe it. How awfully sudden! "Is it apoplexy?" I asked, lifting my head.

"No, I should say not."

"Then what is it?"

"I cannot tell; it may be the heart."

"Are you sure he is dead? Beyond all hope?"

"He is indeed."

A disagreeable doubt rushed over my mind, and I spoke on the impulse of the moment. "Has he come by his death fairly?"

The surgeon paused before he answered. "I see no reason, as yet, to infer otherwise. There are no signs of violence about him."

I cannot describe my feelings as we stood looking down at him. Never had I felt so before. What was I to do next?—how act? A hazy idea was making itself heard that some weighty responsibility lay upon me.

Just then a cab dashed up to the door; we heard it all too plainly in the hushed silence; and someone knocked and rang. Lennard went down to open it, and I told him to send in the policeman and fetch another doctor. Looking over the banisters I saw George Coney come in.

"Such a downfall to my plans, Mr. Strange," he began, seeing me as he ascended the stairs. "I went round to my inn to brush myself up before going to the play, and there I found a letter from my father, which they had forgotten to give me this morning. Our bailiff's been taken ill, cannot leave his bed, and father writes that I had better let the horse and the thirty pounds go for a bad job, and come home, for he can't have me away longer. So my spree's done for, this time, and I am on my way to the station, to catch the nine o'clock train."

"Don't go in until you have heard what is there," I whispered, as he was entering the room. "Mr. Brightman, whom you left well, is lying on the floor, and——"

"And what?" asked young Coney, looking at me.

"I fear he is dead."

After a dismayed pause he went gently into the room, taking off his hat reverently and treading on tiptoe. "Poor fellow! poor gentleman!" he uttered, after looking at him. "What an awful thing! How was he taken?"

"We do not know how. He was alone."

"What, alone when he was taken! no one to help him!" returned the young man. "That was hard! What has he died of?"

"Probably the heart," interposed Dr. Dickenson.

"Last summer a carter of ours fell down as he was standing near us; my father was giving him directions about a load of hay, and when we picked him up he was dead," spoke the young man. "That was the heart, they said. But he looked calm and quiet, not as Mr. Brightman looks. He left seven children, poor chap!"

At that juncture Mr. Lennard returned with the policeman. Another doctor, he said, would be round directly. After some general conversation, George Coney looked at his watch.

"Mr. Strange, my time's up. Would it be convenient to give me that money again? I should like to take it down with me, you see, just to have the laugh against the old folks at home."

"I will give it you," I said.

But for the very life of me, I could not put my hand into the dead man's pocket. I beckoned to Lennard. "Can you take out his keys?"

"Let me do it," said Dr. Dickenson, for Lennard did not seem to relish the task either. "I am more accustomed to death than you are. Which pocket are they in?"

"The right-hand pocket of his trousers; he always kept them there," was my answer.

Dr. Dickenson found the keys and handed them to me. I unlocked the drawer, being obliged to bend over the dead to do so, and young Coney stepped forward to receive the bag.

But the bag was not there.

CHAPTER IV.
LEAH'S STORY.

OUR dismayed faces might have formed a study for a painter, as we stood in my room in Essex Street: the doctor, George Coney, Lennard and myself. On the floor, between the hearthrug and the desk, lay the dead man, the blaze of the fire and the gaslights playing on his features. Mr. Brightman was dead. In my mental pain and emotion I could not realize the fact; would not believe that it was true. He had died thus suddenly, no one near him; no one, so far as was yet known, in the house at the time. And to me, at least, there seemed to be some mystery attaching to it.

But, at this particular moment, we were looking for George Coney's sovereigns, which Mr. Brightman, not much more than an hour before, had locked up in the deep drawer of his desk, returning the keys to his pocket. After Dr. Dickenson had handed me the keys I unlocked and opened the drawer. But the bag was not there.

If the desk itself had disappeared, I could not have been more surprised. Lying in the drawer, close to where the bag had been, was a gold watch belonging to Mrs. Brightman, which had been brought up to town to be cleaned. That was undisturbed. "Coney," I exclaimed, "the money is not here."

"It was put there," replied young Coney. "Next to that watch."

"I know it was," I answered. I opened the drawer on the other side, but that was full of papers. I looked about on the desk; then on my own desk, even unlocking the drawers, though I had had the key in my own pocket; then on the tables and mantelpiece. Not a trace could I see of the canvas bag.

"What bag is it?" inquired Dr. Dickenson, who, of course, had known nothing of this. "What was in it?"

"A small canvas bag containing some gold that Mr. George Coney had wished to leave here until Monday," I answered.

"'Twas one of our sample barley bags; I happened to have it in my pocket when I left home," explained the young man. "My father's initials were on it: S. C."

"How much was in it?" asked Lennard.

"Thirty pounds."

"I fear you will be obliged to go without it, after all," I said, when I had turned everything over, "for it is not to be found. I will remit you thirty pounds on Monday. We send our spare cash to the bank on Saturday afternoons, so that I have not so much in the house: and I really do not know where Mr. Brightman has put the cheque-book. It is strange that he should have taken the bag out of the drawer again."

"Perhaps it may be in one of his pockets," suggested the doctor. "Shall I search them?"

"No, no," interposed George Coney. "I wouldn't have the poor gentleman disturbed just for that. You'll remit it to me, Mr. Strange. Not to my father," he added, with a smile: "to me."

I went down with him, and there sat Leah at the bottom of the stairs, leaning her head against the banisters, almost under the hall lamp. "When did you come in, Leah?" I asked.

She rose hastily, and faced me. "I thought you were out, sir. I have come in only this instant."

"What is the matter?" I continued, struck with the white, strange look upon her face. "Are you ill?"

"No, sir, not ill. Trouble is the lot of us all."

I shook hands with George Coney as he got into his cab and departed, and then returned indoors. Leah was hastening along the passage to the kitchen stairs. I called her back again. "Leah," I said, "do you know what has happened to Mr. Brightman?"

"No, sir," answered she. "What has happened to him?"

"You must prepare for a shock. He is dead."

She had a cloth and a plate in her hand, and laid them down on the slab as she backed against the wall, staring in horror. Then her features relaxed into a wan smile.

"Ah, Master Charles, you are thinking to be a boy again to-night, and are playing a trick upon me, as you used to do in the old days, sir."

"I wish to my heart it was so, Leah. Mr. Brightman is lying upon the floor in my room. I fear there can be no doubt that he is dead."

"My poor master!" she slowly ejaculated. "Heaven have mercy upon him!— and upon us! Why, it's not more than three-quarters of an hour since I took up some water to him."

"Did he ask for it?"

"He rang the bell, sir, and asked for a decanter of water and a tumbler."

"How did he look then, Leah? Where was he sitting?"

"He was sitting at his table, sir, and he looked as usual, for all I saw, but his head was bent over something he was reading. I put some coals on the fire and came away. Mr. Charles, who is up there with him?"

"Dr. Dickenson and——"

A knock at the door interrupted me. It proved to be the other doctor I had sent for.

The medical men proceeded to examine Mr. Brightman more closely. I had sent for the police, and they also were present. I then searched his pockets, a policeman aiding me, and we put their contents carefully away. But there was no bag containing gold amongst them. How had it disappeared?

A most unhappy circumstance was the fact that I could not send for Mrs. Brightman, for I did not know where she was. Mr. Brightman had said she was out of town, but did not say where.

When Watts came home, I despatched him to the house at Clapham, allowing him no time to indulge his grief or his curiosity. Leah had knelt down by Mr. Brightman, tears silently streaming from her eyes.

The fire in the front room was relighted; the fire, the very coals, which he, poor man, had so recently taken off; and I, Lennard and Arthur Lake went in there to talk the matter over quietly.

"Lennard," I said, "I am not satisfied that he has died a natural death. I hope——"

"There are no grounds for any other supposition, Mr. Strange," he interrupted. "None whatever. *Are* there?" he added, looking at me.

"I trust there are none—but I don't quite like the attendant circumstances of the case. The loss of that bag of money causes all sorts of unpleasant suspicions to arise. When you came to the house, Lennard, did you go straight upstairs?" I added, after a pause.

"No, I went into the front office," replied Lennard. "I thought Sir Edmund Clavering might still be here."

"Was Leah out or in?"

"Leah was standing at the front door, looking—as it seemed to me—down the steps leading to the Thames. While I was lighting my candle by the hall-lamp, she shut the front door and came to me. She was extremely agitated, and——"

"Agitated?" I interrupted.

"Yes," said Lennard; "I could not be mistaken. I stared at her, wondering what could cause it, and why her face was so white—almost as white as Mr. Brightman's is now. She asked—as earnestly as if she were pleading for life—whether I would stop in the house for a few minutes, as Mr. Brightman had not gone, while she ran out upon an errand. I inquired whether Sir Edmund Clavering was upstairs, and she said no; he had left; Mr. Strange was out, and Mr. Brightman was alone."

"Did she go out?"

"Immediately," replied Lennard; "just as she was, without bonnet or shawl. I went up to your room, and tapped at the door. It was not answered, and I went in. At first I thought the room was empty; but in a moment I saw Mr. Brightman lying on the ground. He was dead even then; I am certain of it," added Lennard, pausing from natural emotion. "I raised his head, and put a little water to his temples, but I saw that he was dead."

"It is an awful thing!" exclaimed Lake.

"I can tell you that I thought so," assented Lennard. "I knew that the first thing must be to get in a doctor; but how I found my way up the street to Dickenson's I hardly remember. No wonder I left the front door open behind me."

I turned all this over in my mind. There were two points I did not like— Leah's agitation, and Lennard's carelessness in leaving the door open. I called in one of the policemen from the other room, for they were there still, with the medical men.

"Williams," I began, "you saw me come down the street with my latch-key in my hand?"

"I did, sir, and wished you good-evening," replied Williams. "It wasn't long after the other gentleman," indicating Lennard, "had run out."

"I did not see you," cried Lennard, looking at him. "I wish I had seen you. I wanted help, and there was not a soul in the street."

"I was standing in shadow, at the top of the steps leading to the water," said the man. "You came out, sir, all in a hurry, and went rushing up the street, leaving the door open."

"And it is that door's having been left open that I don't like," I observed. "If this money does not turn up, I can only think some rogue got in and took it."

"Nobody got in, sir," said the policeman. "I had my eye on the door the whole time till you came down. To see two folk running like mad out of a quiet and respectable house roused my suspicions; and I went up to the door and stood near it till you entered."

"How did you see two running out of it?" I inquired. "There was only Mr. Lennard."

"I had seen somebody before that—a woman," replied the officer. "She came out, and went tearing down the steps towards the river, calling to someone out of sight. I think it was your servant, Mrs. Watts, but I was only half-way down the street then, and she was too quick for me."

"Then you are quite sure no one entered?"

"Quite sure, sir. I never moved from the door."

"Setting aside Williams's testimony, there was scarcely time for anyone to get in and do mischief," observed Lake. "And no one could take that gold without first getting the keys out of Mr. Brightman's pocket," he rejoined. "For such a purpose, who would dare rifle the pockets of the dead?"

"And then replace the keys," added Lennard.

"Besides," I said impulsively, "no one knew the money was there. Mr. Brightman, myself, and George Coney were alone cognisant of the fact. The more one thinks of it, the stranger it seems to grow."

The moments passed. The doctors and the police had gone away, and nothing remained but the sad burden in the next room. Lennard also left me to go home, for there was nothing more to be done; and Arthur Lake, who had gone round to his rooms, came in again. His conscience was smiting him, he said, for having deserted me. We sat down in the front room, as before, and began to discuss the mystery. I remarked, to begin with, that there existed not the slightest loophole of suspicion to guide us.

"Except one," said Lake quietly. "And I may pain you, Charley, if I venture to suggest it."

"Nonsense!" I cried. "How could it pain me? Unless you think I took it myself!"

"I fancy it was Leah."

"Leah?"

"Well, I do. She was the only person in the house, except Mr. Brightman. And what did her agitation mean—the agitation Lennard has referred to?"

"No, no, Arthur; it could not have been Leah. Admitting the doubt for a moment, how could she have done it?"

"Only in this way. I have been arguing it out with myself in my rooms: and of course it may be all imagination. Leah took up some water, she says, that Mr. Brightman rang for. Now, it may be that he had the drawer open and she saw the money. Or it may even be that, for some purpose or other, he had the bag upon the table. Was he taken ill whilst she was in the room? and did she, overcome by temptation, steal the money? I confess that this possibility presents itself forcibly to me," concluded Lake. "Naturally she would afterwards be in a state of agitation."

I sat revolving what he said, but could not bring my mind to admit it. Circumstances—especially her agitation—might seem to tell against her, but I believed the woman to be honest as the day.

There is not the slightest doubt that almost every man born into the world is adapted for one especial calling over all others; and it is an unhappy fact that this peculiar tendency is very rarely discovered and followed up. It is the misdirection of talent which causes so many of the failures in life. In my own case this mistake had not occurred. I believe that of all pursuits common to man, I was by nature most fitted for that of a solicitor. At the Bar, as a pleader, I should have failed, and ruined half the clients who entrusted me with briefs. But for penetration, for seizing without effort the different points of a case laid before me, few equalled me. I mention this only because it is a fact: not from motives of self-praise and vanity. Vanity? I am only thankful that my talents were directed into their proper channel. And this judgment, exercised now, told me that Leah was not guilty. I said so to Arthur Lake.

The return of Watts interrupted us. He had brought back with him Mr. Brightman's butler, Perry—a respectable, trustworthy man, who had been long in the family. I shall never forget his emotion as he stood over his dead master, to whom he was much attached. Mrs. and Miss Brightman had gone to Hastings for two or three days, he said, and I determined to go there in the morning and break the sad tidings to them.

Sad tidings, indeed; a grievous calamity for us all. That night I could not sleep, and in the morning I rose unrefreshed. The doubt about Leah and the money also troubled me. Though in one sense convinced that she could not have done it, the possibility that she might be guilty kept presenting itself before me.

She came into the room while I was at breakfast—earlier than I need have been, so far as the train was concerned—and I detained her for a moment.

Very spruce and neat she looked this morning.

"Leah," I began, "there is an unpleasant mystery attending this affair."

"As to what Mr. Brightman has died of, sir?"

"I do not allude to that. But there is some money missing."

"Money!" echoed Leah, in what looked like genuine surprise.

"Last night, after Mr. Brightman came in from dinner, he put a small canvas bag, containing thirty pounds in gold, in the deep drawer of his desk in my room, locked it and put the keys in his pocket. I had occasion to look for that gold immediately after he was found dead, and it was gone."

"Bag and all?" said Leah, after a pause.

"Bag and all."

"Not stolen, surely?"

"I don't see how else it can have disappeared. It could not go without hands; and the question is, did anyone get into the house and take it?"

She looked at me, and I at her: she was apparently thinking. "But how could anyone get in, sir?" she asked in tones of remonstrance.

"I do not see how, unless it was when you went out, Leah. You were out some time, you know. You ran out of the house and down the steps leading to the river, and you were in great agitation. What did it mean?"

Leah threw up her hands in distress. "Oh, Mr. Charles!" she gasped. "Please don't question me, sir. I cannot tell you anything about that."

"I must know it, Leah."

She shook her head. Her tears had begun to fall.

"Indeed you must explain it to me," I continued, speaking gently. "There is no help for it. Don't you see that this will have to be investigated, and——"

"You never suspect me of taking the money, sir?" she exclaimed breathlessly.

"No, I do not," I replied firmly. "It is one thing to be sure of honesty, and quite another thing to wish mysterious circumstances cleared up, where the necessity for doing so exists. What was your mystery last night, Leah?"

"Must I tell you, sir?"

"Indeed you must. I dare say to tell it will not hurt you, or to hear it hurt me."

"I would die rather than Watts should know of it," she exclaimed, in low, impassioned tones, glancing towards the door.

"Watts is in the kitchen, Leah, and cannot hear you. Speak out."

"I never committed but one grave fault in my life," she began, "and that was telling a deliberate lie. The consequences have clung to me ever since, and if things go on as they are going on now, they'll just drive me into the churchyard. When I lived with your people I was a young widow, as you may remember, sir; but perhaps you did not know that I had a little child. Your mamma knew it, but I don't think the servants did, for I was never one to talk of my own affairs. Just your age, Master Charles, was my little Nancy, and when her father died his sister took to her; old Miss Williams— for she was a deal older than him. She had a bit of a farm in Dorsetshire, and I'm afraid Nancy had to work hard at it. But it failed after a time, and Miss Williams died; and Nancy, then about seventeen, had come, I heard, to London. I was at Dover then, not long returned from abroad, and was just married to James Watts; and I found—I found," Leah dropped her voice, "that Nancy had gone wrong. Someone had turned her brain with his vows and his promises, and she had come up to London with him."

"Why don't you sit down whilst you talk, Leah?"

"I had told Watts I had no children," she continued, disregarding my injunction. "And that was the lie, Mr. Charles. More than once he had said in my hearing that he would never marry a ready-made family. For very shame I could not tell him, when I found how things were with Nancy. After we came to London, I searched her out and went to her in secret, begging her to leave the man, but she would not."

A burst of emotion stopped Leah. She soon resumed:

"She would not leave him. In spite of all I could say or do, though I went down on my knees to her, and sobbed and prayed my heart out, she remained with him. And she is with him still."

"All this time?"

"All this time, sir; seven years. He was once superior to her in position, but he has fallen from it now, is unsteady, and drinks half his time away. Sometimes he is in work; oftener without it; and the misery and privation she goes through no tongue can tell. He beats her, abuses her——"

"Why does she not leave him?"

"Ah, sir, why don't we do many things that we ought? Partly because she's afraid he would keep the children. There are three of them. Many a time she would have died of hunger but for me. I help her all I can; she's my own child. Sir, you asked me, only yesterday, why I went shabby; but, instead of buying clothes for myself, I scrape and save to keep her poor body and soul together. I go without food to take it to her; many a day I put my dinner away, telling Watts I don't feel inclined for it then and will eat it by-and-by. He thinks I do so. She does not beg of me; she has never entered this house; she has never told that tyrant of hers that I am her mother. 'Mother,' she has said to me, 'never fear. I would rather die than bring trouble on you.'"

"But about last night?" I interrupted.

"I was at work in the kitchen when a little gravel was thrown against the window. I guessed who it was, and went up to the door. If Watts had been at home, I should have taken no notice, but just have said, 'Drat those street boys again!' or something of that sort. There she was, leaning against the opposite railings, and she crossed over when she saw me. She said she was beside herself with misery and trouble, and I believe she was. He had been beating her, and she had not tasted food since the previous day; not a crumb. She kept looking towards the steps leading to the Thames, and I thought she might have got it in her head, what with her weak condition of body and her misery of mind, to put an end to herself. I tried, sir, to soothe and reason with her; what else could I do? I said I would fetch her some food, and give her sevenpence to buy a loaf to take home to her children."

"Where does she live?" I interposed.

"In this parish, St. Clement Danes; and there are some parts of this parish, you know, sir, as bad as any in London. When I offered to fetch her food, she said, No, she would not take it; her life was too wretched to bear, and she should end it; she had come out to do so. It was just what I feared. I scolded her. I told her to stay there at the door, and I shut it and ran down for the food. But when I got back to the door, I couldn't see her anywhere. Then I heard a voice from the steps call out 'Good-bye!' and I knew she was going to the water. At that moment Mr. Lennard came up, and I asked him to remain in the house whilst I went out for a minute. I was almost frightened out of my senses."

"Did you find her?"

"I found her, sir, looking down at the river. I reasoned her into a little better mood, and she ate a little of the food, and I brought her back up the steps, gave her the sevenpence, and led her up the street and across the Strand, on her way home. And that's the whole truth, Mr. Charles, of what took me out last night; and I declare I know no more of the missing money than a babe unborn. I had just come back with the empty plate and cloth when you saw me sitting on the stairs."

The whole truth I felt sure it was. Every word, every look of Leah's proclaimed it.

"And that's my sad secret," she added; "one I have to bear about with me at all times, in my work and out of my work. Watts is a good husband to me, but he prides himself on his respectability, and I wouldn't have him know that I have deceived him for the universe. I wouldn't have him know that *she*, being what she is, was my daughter. He said he'd treat me to Ashley's Circus last winter, and gave me two shillings, and I pretended to go. But I gave it to her, poor thing, and walked about in the cold, looking at the late shops, till it was time to come home. Watts asked me what I had seen, and I told him such marvels that he said he'd go the next night himself, for he had never heard the like, and he supposed it must be a benefit night. You will not tell him my secret, sir?"

"No, Leah, I will not tell him. It is safe with me."

With a long drawn sigh she turned to leave the room. But I stopped her.

"A moment yet, Leah. Can you remember at what time you took up the water to Mr. Brightman?"

"It was some time before the stone came to the window. About ten minutes, maybe, sir, after you went out. I heard you come downstairs whistling, and go out."

"No one came to the house during my absence?"

"No one at all, sir."

"Did you notice whether Mr. Brightman had either of the drawers of his desk open when you took up the water?"

Leah shook her head. "I can't say, sir," she answered. "I did not notice one way or the other."

CHAPTER V.

LADY CLAVERING.

THE people were coming out of the various churches when I reached Hastings. Going straight to the Queen's Hotel, I asked for Mrs. Brightman. Perry had said she was staying there. It was, I believe, the only good hotel in the place in those days. Hatch, Mrs. Brightman's maid, came to me at once. Her mistress was not yet up, she said, having a bad headache.

Hatch and I had become quite confidential friends during these past years. She was not a whit altered since I first saw her, and to me did not look a day older. The flaming ringlets adorned her face as usual, and sky-blue cap-strings flowed behind them this morning. Hatch was glaringly plain; Hatch had a wonderful tongue, and was ever ready to exercise it, and Hatch's diction and grammar were unique; nevertheless, you could not help liking Hatch.

But to hear that Mrs. Brightman was ill in bed rather checkmated me. I really did not know what to do.

"My business with your mistress is of very great importance, Hatch," I observed. "I ought to see her. I have come down on purpose to see her."

"You might see her this afternoon, Mr. Charles; not before," spoke Hatch decisively. "These headaches is uncommon bad while they last. Perhaps Miss Annabel would do? She is not here, though; but is staying with her aunt Lucy."

"I have brought down bad news, Hatch. I should not like Miss Annabel to be the first to hear it."

"Bad news!" repeated Hatch quickly, as she stared at me with her great green eyes. "Our house ain't burnt down, surely! Is that the news, sir?"

"Worse than that, Hatch. It concerns Mr. Brightman."

Hatch's manner changed in a moment. Her voice became timid. "For goodness' sake, Mr. Charles! he is not ill, is he?"

"Worse, Hatch. He is dead," I whispered.

Hatch backed to a chair and dropped into it: we were in Mrs. Brightman's sitting-room. "The Lord be good to us!" she exclaimed, in all reverence. Her red cheeks turned white, her eloquence for once deserted her.

I sat down and gave her the details in a few brief words: she was a confidential, trusted servant, and had lived with her mistress many years. It affected her even more than I had expected. She wrung her hands, her tears coursed freely.

"My poor master—my poor mistress!" she exclaimed. "What on earth— Mr. Charles, is it *sure* he is dead? quite dead?" she broke off to ask.

"Nay, Hatch, I have told you."

Presently she got up, and seemed to rally her courage. "Anyway, Mr. Charles, we shall have to meet this, and deal with it as we best may. I mean the family, sir, what's left of 'em. And missis must be told—and, pardon me, sir, but I think I'd best be the one to tell her. She is so used to me, you see," added Hatch, looking at me keenly. "She might take it better from me than from you; that is, it might seem less hard."

"Indeed, I should be only too glad to be spared the task," was my answer.

"But you must tell Miss Brightman, sir, and Miss Annabel. Perhaps if you were to go now, Mr. Charles, while I do the best I can with my missis, we might be ready for the afternoon train. That, you say, will be best to travel by——"

"I said the train would be the best of the trains to-day, Hatch. It is for Mrs. Brightman to consider whether she will go up to-day or to-morrow."

"Well, yes, Mr. Charles, that's what I mean. My head's almost moithered. But I think she is sure to go up to-day."

Miss Brightman, who was Mr. Brightman's only sister, lived in a handsome house facing the sea. Annabel visited her a good deal, staying with her sometimes for weeks together. Mr. Brightman had sanctioned it, Mrs. Brightman did not object to it.

Upon reaching the house, the footman said Miss Brightman was not yet in from church, and ushered me into the drawing-room. Annabel was there. And really, like Hatch, she was not much altered, except in height and years, since the day I first saw her, when she had chattered to me so freely and lent me her favourite book, "The Old English Baron." She was fourteen then: a graceful, pretty child, with charming manners; her dark brown eyes, sweet and tender and bright like her father's, her features delicately carved like her mother's, a rose-blush on her dimpled cheeks. She was twenty now, and a graceful, pretty woman. No, not one whit altered.

She was standing by the fire in her silk attire, just as she had come in from church, only her bonnet-strings untied. Bonnets were really bonnets then, and rendered a lovely face all the more attractive. Annabel's bonnet that day was pink, and its border intermingled, as it seemed, with the waves of her soft brown hair. She quite started with surprise.

"Is it *you*, Charley!" she exclaimed, coming forward, the sweet rose-blush deepening and the sweet eyes brightening. "Have you come to Hastings? Is papa with you?"

"No, Annabel, he is not with me," I answered gravely, as I clasped her hand. "I wanted to see Miss Brightman."

"She will be here directly. She called in to see old Mrs. Day, who is ill: a great friend of Aunt Lucy's. Did papa——"

But we were interrupted by the return of Miss Brightman, a small, fragile woman, with delicate lungs. Annabel left us together.

How I accomplished my unhappy task I hardly knew. How Miss Brightman subsequently imparted it to Annabel I did not know at all. It must be enough to say that we went to London by an afternoon train, bearing our weight of care. All, except Miss Brightman. Hatch travelled in the carriage with us.

In appearance, at any rate, the news had most affected Mrs. Brightman. Her frame trembled, her pale face and restless hands twitched with nervousness. Of course, her headache went for something.

"I have them so very badly," she moaned to me once during the journey. "They unfit me for everything."

And, indeed, these headaches of Mrs. Brightman's were nothing new to me. She had always suffered from them. But of late, that is to say during the past few months, when by chance I went to Clapham, I more often than not found her ill and invisible from this distressing pain. My intimacy with Mrs. Brightman had not made much progress. The same proud, haughty woman she was when I first saw her, she had remained. Coldly civil to me, as to others; and that was all that could be said.

When about half-way up, whilst waiting for an express to pass, or something of that sort, and we were for some minutes at a standstill, I told Mrs. Brightman about the missing money belonging to George Coney.

"It is of little consequence if it be lost," was her indifferent and no doubt thoughtless comment. "What is thirty pounds?"

Little, I knew, to a firm like ours, but the uncertainty it left us in was a great deal. "Setting aside the mystery attaching to the loss," I remarked, "there remains a suspicion that we may have a thief about us; and that is not a pleasant feeling. Other things may go next."

Upon reaching London we drove to Essex Street. What a painful visit it was! Even now I cannot bear to think of it. Poor Mrs. Brightman grew nervously excited. As she looked down upon him, in his death-stillness, I thought she would have wept her heart away. Annabel strove to be calm for her mother's sake.

After some tea, which Leah and Hatch brought up to us, I saw them safely to Clapham, and then returned home.

Monday morning rose, and its work with it: the immediate work connected with our painful loss, and the future work that was to fall upon me. The chief weight and responsibility of the business had hitherto been his share; now it must be all mine. In the course of the day I sent a cheque to George Coney.

An inquest had to be held, and took place early on Tuesday morning. Mr. Brightman's death was proved, beyond doubt, to have occurred from natural causes, though not from disease of the heart. He had died by the visitation of God. But for the disappearance of the money, my thoughts would never have dwelt on any other issue.

After it was over, Lennard was standing with me in the front-room, from which the jury had just gone out, when we fell to talking about the missing money and its unaccountable loss. It lay heavily upon my mind. Fathom it I could not, turn it about as I would. Edgar Lennard was above suspicion, and he was the only one, so far as he and I knew, who had been in the room after the bag was put there, Leah excepted. Of her I felt equally certain. Lennard began saying how heartily he wished he had not been told to come back that night; but I requested him to be at ease, for he had quite as much reason to suspect me, as I him.

"Not quite," answered he, smiling; "considering that you had to make it good."

"Well, Lennard, I dare say the mystery will be solved some time or other. Robberies, like murders, generally come out. The worst is, we cannot feel assured that other losses may not follow."

"Not they," returned Lennard, too confidently. "This one has been enough for us."

"Did it ever strike you, Lennard, that Mr. Brightman had been in failing health lately?"

"Often," emphatically spoke Lennard. "I think he had something on his mind."

"On his mind? I should say it was on his health. There were times when he seemed to have neither energy nor spirits for anything. You don't know how much business he has of late left to me that he used to do himself."

"Well," contended Lennard, "it used to strike me he was not at ease; that something or other was troubling him."

"Yes, and now that this fatal termination has ensued, we see that the trouble may have been health," I maintained. "Possibly he knew that something was dangerously wrong with him."

"Possibly so," conceded Lennard.

He was leaving the room for his own, when a clerk met him and said that Sir Edmund Clavering was asking for Mr. Strange. I bade him show up Sir Edmund.

Mr. Brightman had for years been confidential solicitor to Sir Ralph Clavering, a physician, whose baronetcy was a new one. When Sir Ralph gave up practice, and retired to an estate he bought in the country, a Mrs. Clavering, a widow, whose husband had been a distant cousin of Sir Ralph's, entered it with him as his companion and housekeeper. It ended in his marrying her, as these companionships so often end, especially where the man is old, and the woman young, attractive and wily. Mrs. Clavering was poor, and no doubt played for the stake she won. The heir-presumptive to Sir Ralph's title was his nephew, Edmund Clavering, but his fortune he could leave to whom he would.

Sir Ralph Clavering died—only about ten days before Mr. Brightman's own death. The funeral took place on the Tuesday—this very day week of which I am writing. After attending it, Mr. Brightman returned to the office in the evening. The clerks had left, and he came up to my room.

"Take this off my hat, will you, Charles?" he said. "I can't go home in it, of course: and Mrs. Brightman had a superstition against hat-scarves going into the house."

I undid the black silk and laid it on the table. "What am I to do with it, sir?"

"Anything. Give it to Leah for a Sunday apron. My lady treated us to a specimen of her temper when the will was read," he added. "She expected to inherit all, and is not satisfied with the competency left to her."

"Who does inherit?" I asked: for Mr. Brightman had never enlightened me, although I knew that he had made Sir Ralph's will.

"Edmund Clavering. And quite right that he should do so: the estate ought to go with the title. Besides, setting aside that consideration, Sir Edmund is

- 45 -

entitled to it quite as much as my lady. More so, I think. There's the will, Charles; you can read it."

I glanced over the will, which Mr. Brightman had brought back with him. Lady Clavering had certainly a competency, but the bulk of the property was left to Sir Edmund, the inheritor of the title. I was very much surprised.

"I thought she would have had it all, Mr. Brightman. Living estranged as Sir Ralph did from his brother, even refusing to be reconciled when the latter was dying, the estrangement extended to the son, Edmund, I certainly thought Lady Clavering would have come in for all. You thought so too, sir."

"I did, until I made the will. And at one time it was Sir Ralph's intention to leave most of it to her. But for certain reasons which arose, he altered his plans. Sufficient reasons," added Mr. Brightman, in a marked, emphatic manner. "He imparted them to me when he gave instructions for his will. I should have left her less."

"May I know them?"

"No, Charles. They were told to me in confidence, and they concern neither you nor me. Is the gas out in the next room?"

"Yes. Shall I light it?"

"It is not worth while. That hand-lamp of yours will do. I only want to put up the will."

I took the lamp, and lighted Mr. Brightman into the front room, his own exclusively. He opened the iron safe, and there deposited Sir Ralph Clavering's will, to be left there until it should be proved.

That is sufficient explanation for the present. Sir Edmund Clavering, shown up by Lennard himself, came into the room. I had never acted for him; Mr. Brightman had invariably done so.

"Can you carry my business through, Mr. Strange?" he asked, after expressing his shock and regret at Mr. Brightman's sudden fate.

"I hope so. Why not, Sir Edmund?"

"You have not Mr. Brightman's legal knowledge and experience."

"Not his experience, certainly; because he was an old man and I am a young one. But, as far as practice goes, I have for some time had chief control of the business. Mr. Brightman almost confined himself to seeing clients. You may trust me, Sir Edmund."

"Oh yes, I dare say it will be all right," he rejoined. "Do you know that Lady Clavering and her cousin John—my cousin also—mean to dispute the will?"

"Upon what grounds?"

"Upon Sir Ralph's incompetency to make one, I suppose—as foul a plea as ever false woman or man invented. Mr. Brightman can prove—— Good heavens! every moment I forget that he is dead," broke off Sir Edmund. "How unfortunate that he should have gone just now!"

"But there cannot fail to be ample proof of Sir Ralph's competency. The servants about him must know that he was of sane and healthy mind."

"I don't know what her schemes may be," rejoined Sir Edmund; "but I do know that she will not leave a stone unturned to wrest my rights from me. I am more bitter than gall and wormwood to her."

"Because you have inherited most of the money."

"Ay, for one thing. But there's another reason, more galling to her even than that."

Sir Edmund looked at me with a peculiar expression. He was about my own age, and would have been an exceedingly pleasant man but for his pride. When he could so far forget that as to throw it off, he was warm and cordial.

"Her ladyship is a scheming woman, Mr. Strange. She flung off into a fit of resentment at first, which Mr. Brightman witnessed, but very shortly her tactics changed. Before Sir Ralph had been three days in his grave, she contrived to intimate to me that we had better join interests. Do you understand?"

I did not know whether to understand or not. It was inconceivable.

"And I feel ashamed to enlighten you," said Sir Edmund passionately. "She offered herself to me; my willing wife. 'If you will wed no other woman, I will wed no other man——' How runs the old ballad? Not in so many words, but in terms sufficiently plain to be deciphered. I answered as plainly, and declined. Declined to join interests—declined *her*—and so made her my mortal enemy for ever. Do you know her?"

"I never saw her."

"Take care of yourself, then, should you be brought into contact with her," laughed Sir Edmund. "She is a Jezebel. All the same, she is one of the most fascinating of women: irresistibly so, no doubt, to many people. Had she been any but my uncle's wife—widow—I don't know how it might have gone with me. By the way, Mr. Strange, did Mr. Brightman impart to you Sir Ralph's reason for devising his property to me? He had always said, you know, that he would not do it. Mr. Brightman would not tell me the reason for the change."

"No, he did not. Sir Ralph intended, I believe, to bequeath most of it to his wife, and altered his mind quite suddenly. So much Mr. Brightman told me."

"Found out Jezebel, perhaps, at some trick or other."

That I thought all too likely; but did not say so. Sir Edmund continued to speak a little longer upon business matters, and then rose.

"The will had better be proved without delay," he paused to say.

"I will see about it the first thing next week, Sir Edmund. It would have been done this week but for Mr. Brightman's unexpected death."

"Why do you sink your voice to a whisper?" asked Sir Edmund, as we were quitting the room. "Do you fear eavesdroppers?"

I was not conscious that I had sunk it, until recalled to the fact. "Every time I approach this door," I said, pointing to the one opening into the other room, "I feel as if I were in the presence of the dead. He is still lying there."

"What—Mr. Brightman?"

"It is where he died. He will be removed to his late residence to-night."

"I think I will see him," cried Sir Edmund, laying his hand on the door.

"As you please. I would not advise you." And he apparently thought better of it, and went down.

I had to attend the Vice-Chancellor's Court; law business goes on without respect to the dead. Upon my return in the afternoon, I was in the front office, speaking to Lennard, when a carriage drove down the street, and stopped at the door. Our blinds were down, but one of the clerks peeped out. "A gentleman's chariot, painted black," he announced: "the servants in deep mourning."

Allen went out and brought back a card. "The lady wishes to see you, sir."

I cast my eyes on it—"Lady Clavering." And an involuntary smile crossed my face, at the remembrance of Sir Edmund's caution, should I ever be brought into contact with her. But what could Lady Clavering want with me?

She was conducted upstairs, and I followed, leaving my business with Lennard until afterwards. She was already seated in the very chair that, not two hours ago, had held her opponent, Sir Edmund: a very handsome woman, dressed as coquettishly as her widow's weeds allowed. Her face was beautiful as to form and colouring, but its free and vain expression spoiled it. Every glance of her coal-black eye, every movement of her head and hands, every word that fell from her lips, was a purposed display of her charms, a demand for admiration. Sir Edmund need not have cautioned me to keep heart-whole. One so vain and foolish would repel rather than attract me, even though gifted with beauty rarely accorded to woman. A Jezebel? Yes, I agreed with him—a very Jezebel.

"I have the honour of speaking to Mr. Strange? Charles Strange, as I have heard Mr. Brightman call you," she said, with a smile of fascination.

"Yes, I am Charles Strange. What can I do for you, madam?"

"Will you promise to do what I have come to ask you?"

The more she spoke, the less I liked her. I am naturally frank in manner, but I grew reserved with her. "I cannot make a promise without knowing its nature, Lady Clavering."

She picked up her long jet chain, and twirled it about in her fingers. "What a frightfully sudden death Mr. Brightman's has been!" she resumed. "Did he lie ill at all?"

"No. He died suddenly, as he was sitting at his desk. And to render it still more painful, no one was with him."

"I read the account in this morning's paper, and came up at once to see you," resumed Lady Clavering. "He was my husband's confidential adviser. Were you in his confidence also?"

I presumed that she meant Mr. Brightman's, and answered accordingly. "Partially so."

"You are aware how very unjustly my poor childish husband strove to will away his property. Of course the will cannot be allowed to stand. At the time of Sir Ralph's funeral, I informed Mr. Brightman that I should take some steps to assert my rights, and I wished him to be my solicitor in the matter. But no; he refused, and went over to the enemy, Edmund Clavering."

"We were solicitors to Mr. Edmund Clavering before he came into the title."

"Mr. Brightman was; you never did anything for him," she hastily interrupted; "therefore no obligation can lie on you to act for him now. I want you to act for me, and I have come all this way to request you to do so."

"I cannot do so, Lady Clavering. I have seen Sir Edmund since Mr. Brightman's death, and have undertaken to carry on his business."

"Seen Sir Edmund since Mr. Brightman's death!"

"I have indeed."

She threw herself back in her chair, and looked at me from under her vain eyelids. "Leave him, Mr. Strange; you can easily make an excuse, if you will. Mr. Brightman held all my husband's papers, knew all about his property, and no one is so fitted to act for me as you, his partner. I will make it worth your while."

"What you suggest is impossible, Lady Clavering. We are enlisted in the interests—I speak professionally—of the other side, and have already advised with Sir Edmund as to the steps to be taken in the suit you purpose to enter against him. To leave him for you, after doing so, would be dishonourable and impossible."

She shot another glance at me from those mischievous eyes. "I will make it well worth your while, I repeat, Mr. Strange."

I could look mischievous too, if I pleased; perhaps did on occasion; but she could read nothing in my gaze then, as it met hers, that was not sober as old Time.

"I can only repeat my answer, Lady Clavering."

Not a word spoke she; only made play with her eyes. Did the woman mean to subdue me? Her gaze dropped.

"I have heard Mr. Brightman speak of Charles Strange not only as a thorough lawyer, but as a *gentleman*—very fond of the world's vanities."

"Not very fond, Lady Clavering. Joining in them occasionally, in proper time and place."

"I met you once at a large evening party. It was at old Judge Tartar's," she ran on.

"Indeed!" I answered, not remembering it.

"It was before I married Sir Ralph. You came in with your relative, Serjeant Stillingfar. What a charming man he is! I heard you tell someone you had just come down from Oxford. *Won't* you act for me, Mr. Strange?"

"Indeed, it does not lie in my power."

"Well, I did not think a gentleman"—with another stress upon the word—"would have refused to act on my behalf."

"Lady Clavering must perceive that I have no alternative."

"Who is Edmund Clavering that he should be preferred to me?" she demanded with some vehemence.

"Nay, Lady Clavering, circumstances compel the preference."

A silence ensued, and I glanced at my watch—the lawyer's hint. She did not take it.

"Can you tell me whether, amidst the papers Mr. Brightman held belonging to Sir Ralph, there are any letters of mine?"

"I cannot say."

"Some of my letters, to Sir Ralph and others, are missing, and I think they must have got amongst the papers by mistake. Will you look?"

"I will take an early opportunity of doing so."

"Oh, but I mean now. I want them. Why cannot you search now?"

I did not tell her why. In the first place, most of the Clavering papers were in the room where Mr. Brightman was lying—and there were other reasons also.

"I cannot spare the time, Lady Clavering: I have an appointment out of doors which I must keep. I will search for you in a day or two. But should any letters of yours be here—of which I assure you I am ignorant—you will pardon my intimating that it may not be expedient to give them up."

"What do you mean? Why not?"

"Should they bear at all upon the cause at issue between you and Sir Edmund Clavering——"

"But they don't," she interrupted.

"Then, if they do not, I shall be happy to enclose them to you."

"It is of the utmost consequence to me that I should regain possession of them," she said, with suppressed agitation.

"And, if possible, you shall do so." I rose as I spoke, and waited for her to rise. She did so, but advanced to the window and pulled the blind aside.

"My carriage is not back yet, Mr. Strange. A friend who came up with me has gone to do a commission for herself. It will be here in a few minutes. I suppose I can wait."

I begged her to remain as long as she pleased, but to excuse me, for I was already behind time. She drew up the blind a little and sat down at the window as I left her.

After giving some directions to Lennard, I hastened to keep my appointment, which was at the Temple with a chamber-counsel.

The interview lasted about twenty minutes. As I turned into Essex Street again, Lady Clavering's carriage was bowling up it. I raised my hat, and she bowed to me, leaning before another lady, who sat with her, but she looked white and frightened. What had taken her brilliant colour? At the door, when I reached it, stood the clerks, Lennard amongst them, some with a laugh on their countenances, some looking as white and scared as Lady Clavering.

"Why, what is this?" I exclaimed.

They went back to their desks, and Lennard explained.

"You must have seen Lady Clavering's carriage," he began.

"Yes."

"Just before it came for her, cries and shrieks were heard above; startling shrieks, terrifying us all. We hastened up with one accord, and found that Lady Clavering——"

"Well?" I impatiently cried, looking at Lennard.

"Had gone into the next room, and seen Mr. Brightman," he whispered. "It took three of us to hold her, and it ended with hysterics. Leah came flying from the kitchen, took off her bonnet, and brought some water."

I was sorry to hear it; sorry that any woman should have been exposed to so unpleasant a fright. "But it was her own fault," I said to Lennard. "How could she think of entering a room of which the door was locked?"

"What right had she to attempt to enter it at all, locked or unlocked, I should say, Mr. Strange!" returned Lennard severely. "And the best of it was, she laid the blame upon us, asking what business we had to put dead people into public rooms."

"She is a curious sort of woman, I fancy, Lennard."

And the more I thought of her, the more curious I found her. The door between the two rooms had been locked, and the key was lying in the corner of the mantelpiece. Lady Clavering must have searched for the key before she could open the door and enter the room.

With what motive had she entered it?

CHAPTER VI.
THE MISSING WILL.

MR. BRIGHTMAN was buried on the Thursday, and Mr. Serjeant Stillingfar came up from circuit for the funeral. Three or four other gentlemen attended, and myself. It was all done very quietly. After that the will was read.

He had not left as much money as might have been expected. I suppose the rate at which they lived had absorbed it. Nearly the whole of it was vested in trustees, who would pay the interest to Mrs. Brightman until her death, when it would all descend unconditionally to Annabel. If she married again, one half the yearly income at once went to Annabel. To my surprise, I was left executor. Mr. Brightman had never told me so. Of the two executors originally appointed—for the will had been made many years—one had recently died, and Mr. Brightman had inserted my name in his place. That all the work would fall upon my shoulders I knew, for the other executor had become a confirmed invalid.

With regard to our own articles of partnership, provided for by a recent codicil, they were very favourable to me, though somewhat peculiar. If Mr. Brightman died before I was thirty years of age, two-thirds of the net profits of the business were to be paid to Mrs. Brightman for three years; but if I had passed my thirtieth year when he died, only half the profits would go to her. After the first three years, one-third of the profits would be hers for three years more; and then all would revert to me absolutely.

I wanted some years yet of thirty. But it was an excellent and lucrative practice. Few men fall into so good a thing when they are still young.

"So there you are, Charles, the head of one of the best professional houses in London," remarked my uncle Stillingfar, as he took my arm when we were leaving the house. "Rather different from what your fate might have been, had you carried out your wish of going to the Bar. My boy, you may be thankful that you know nothing of the struggles I had to go through."

"Do you still feel quite well and strong, uncle?" I asked, after a bit.

"Yes, I do, Charles. I suppose you think I am growing old. But I believe I am more capable of work than are many of my juniors who are now on circuit with me. With a sound constitution, never played with, and a temperate way of life, we retain our energies, by God's blessing, to an older age than mine."

That was no doubt true. True also that he must be making heaps of money. I wondered what he meant to do with it. He had been very liberal to me as long as I needed help, but that time was over.

The sad week passed away. On the following Monday I set to professional business in earnest: the previous week had been much given to matters not professional. One of the first things to be attended to was to prove the will of Sir Ralph Clavering, and, in the course of the morning, I unlocked the iron safe in the front room to get it. Nothing was ever placed in that safe but wills and title-deeds, and these were never placed anywhere else. But where this particular will was hiding itself, I could not tell, for I turned over every paper the place contained without coming to it. "More haste less speed," cried I to myself, for I had been doing it in a hurry. "I must have overlooked it."

So I began again and went through the papers carefully, paper by paper. I had not overlooked it, for Sir Ralph's will was certainly not there.

Now, was I awake or dreaming? Was there a fairy in the walls to remove things, or was the house bewitched?—or what was it? I went and examined the Clavering papers, which were in Mr. Brightman's desk in the adjoining room—my room, which had been cleaned and put straight again. But the will was not amongst them. I searched other drawers and desks in vain. Then I called up Lennard.

"Do you know anything of Sir Ralph Clavering's will? I cannot find it."

"It must be in the safe," he replied.

"It is not in the safe. Lennard, this is very strange: first that bag of money, and now the will."

"Oh, but it cannot be," returned Lennard, after a pause. "That the gold went, appears to be too plain, but who would take a will? Money might be a temptation, if any stranger did enter Mr. Brightman's room that night, but——"

"It has been proved almost beyond doubt that no one entered, and yet the money went. Lennard, there's something not canny at work in the house, as the Scotch say."

"Do not think it, Mr. Strange," he replied warmly. "The gold appears to have gone in some mysterious manner, but the will cannot be gone. Depend upon it, it is in the safe."

I had a great respect for Lennard's judgment, but I had as great confidence in my own eyesight. I unlocked the safe again, and, taking out the parchments, one by one, handed them to Lennard that he might read their titles. "There," said I, when we had reached the last; "is the will amongst them?"

Lennard's face had turned grave. "This is very extraordinary!" he exclaimed. "Mr. Brightman would not put it anywhere else."

"He never put a will up in any other place than this since I have been with him, Lennard; and I myself saw him put it in; held the light for him: it was in the evening of last Tuesday week, after he came back from Sir Ralph's funeral. It has gone after the gold."

"No, no," he cried, almost in agitation; "it has not, it has not: I will never believe it."

One very slight hope came to me. Mr. Brightman might have given it into the custody of Sir Edmund Clavering. But then Sir Edmund would surely have said so when he spoke to me about proving the will. The loss of the money was nothing to this, for that had been easily replaced, and there was an end of the matter; but this loss could not be replaced, and there was no knowing what the end would be. It might be little short of ruin to Sir Edmund Clavering, and nothing short of ruin to me: for who would continue to employ a firm liable to lose wills?

I was greatly occupied that day, but the missing will lay upon me as a nightmare, and I forced time for a dash up to Sir Edmund Clavering's hotel in the afternoon, bribing the cabman to double speed. By good luck, I found Sir Edmund in, and inquired if he held possession of the will.

"Mr. Brightman holds the will," he replied. "Held, I should say: I cannot yet speak of him in the past tense, you see. He took it home with him after Sir Ralph's funeral."

"I know he brought it home, Sir Edmund; but I thought it possible he might since then have given it into your possession. I hoped he had, for I cannot find the will. I have searched for it everywhere."

"Not find the will!" he echoed. "Perhaps you have looked in every place but the right one," he added, with a slight laugh. "I can tell you where it is."

"Where?"

"In the iron safe in Mr. Brightman's room."

"It was placed there—we never put wills anywhere else; never—but it is not there now. May I ask how you knew it was there, Sir Edmund?"

"Because on the day but one following the funeral I came to town and had an interview with Mr. Brightman in his room. It was on the Thursday. Perhaps you remember that I was with him that day?"

"Quite well."

"During our consultation we differed in opinion as to a certain clause in the will, and Mr. Brightman took it out of the safe to convince me. He was right, and I was wrong; as, indeed, I might have known, considering that he had made the will. He put it back into the safe at once and locked it up. When are you going to prove the will? It ought to be done now."

"I was going to set about it this very day; but, as I say, I cannot find the will."

"It must be easy enough to find a big parchment like that. If not in the safe, Mr. Brightman must have put it elsewhere. Look in all his pigeon-holes and places."

"I have looked: I have looked everywhere.——— Just as I looked some days before for the bag of sovereigns," I mentally added.

But Sir Edmund Clavering was determined to treat the matter lightly: he evidently attached no importance to it whatever, believing that Mr. Brightman had only changed its place.

I went home again, feeling as uncomfortable as I had ever felt in my life. An undefined idea, a doubt, had flashed into my mind whilst I had been talking to Lennard. Imagination is quicker with me, I know, than with many people; and the moment a thing puzzles me, I must dive into its why and wherefore: its various bearings and phases, probable and improbable, natural and unnatural. This doubt—which I had driven away at the time, had been driving away during my gallop to Sir Edmund's, and whilst I was conversing with him—now grew into suspicion.

Let me explain how I arrived at this suspicion. When I found the will had disappeared from the safe—when I searched and searched in vain—I could only come to the conclusion that it had been stolen. But why was it taken? From what motive? Why should that one particular parchment be abstracted, and the others left? Obviously, it could only have been from interested motives. Now, who had an interest in getting possession of the will—so that it might not be proved and acted upon? Only one person in the whole world—Lady Clavering. And Lady Clavering had been alone in the room where the safe was for nearly half an hour.

If she had obtained possession of the will, there was farewell to our ever getting it again. I saw through her character at that first interview: she was a woman absolutely without scruple.

But how could she have got at it? Even supposing she knew the will was in the iron safe, she could not have opened it without the key; and how could she have obtained the key?

Again—if Lady Clavering were the guilty party, what became of my very natural suspicions that the will and the gold were both taken by the same hand? And with the gold Lady Clavering could have had nothing to do. Look at it as I would, perplexities arose; points difficult, if not impossible, to reconcile.

Lennard met me in the passage on my return. "Is it all right? Has Sir Edmund got it, sir?"

"No, no; I told you it was a forlorn hope. Come upstairs, Lennard. Sir Edmund has not the will," I continued, as we entered the front room. "He says that when he was here last Thursday week, Mr. Brightman had occasion to refer to the will, took it from the safe, and put it back again. Therefore it is since that period that the theft has taken place."

"Can you really look upon it as *stolen*?" Lennard uttered, with emphasis. "Who would steal so valueless a thing as a will?"

"Not valueless to everyone."

"No one in the house would do such a thing. You have a suspicion?" he added.

"Yes, I have, Lennard."

He began to pace the room. Lennard was, in truth, completely upset by this loss. "Of whom?" he presently jerked out. "Surely not of Leah!"

"Of Leah! Oh no!"

"I fancied you suspected her in the matter of the money. I feel sure she was innocent."

"So do I. Leah no more took the money than you or I did, Lennard. And what should she want with the will? If I made her a present of all the wills in the safe, she would only light her fires with them as useless lumber. Try again."

But he only shook his head. "I cannot catch your drift, sir."

"To all persons, two excepted, the will would be as useless as to Leah. One of those two is Sir Edmund; and he has it not: the other is Lady Clavering."

"But surely you cannot suspect her!" exclaimed Lennard. "You cannot suspect Lady Clavering!"

"To say that I suspect her would perhaps be too strong a word, Lennard. If my doubts rest upon her at all, it is because she is the only person who could have an interest in getting possession of the will; and she is the only stranger, as far as I can recollect, who has been alone in this room sufficiently long to take it from the safe."

Lennard was incredulous. "But she had not the key of the safe. She could not have opened it without it."

"I know—I see the improbabilities that encompass my doubts; but I can think of nothing else."

"Where was the key of the safe?" asked Lennard.

"In that back room; and in Mr. Brightman's deep drawer—the drawer from which the gold was taken," was my grave answer. "And she could not have got at it without—without passing him."

Lennard's face grew hot.

"And the key of that drawer was here, in my own pocket, on the bunch." I took out the bunch of keys as I spoke—Mr. Brightman's bunch until within a few days—and shook it before him.

"What mystery has come over the house, about keys, and locks, and things disappearing?" Lennard murmured, as a man bewildered.

"Lennard, it is the question I am asking myself."

"She could never have gone in there and passed him; and stood there while she got the key. A young and beautiful woman like Lady Clavering! Sir, it would be unnatural."

"No more unnatural for beauty than for ugliness, Lennard. Unnatural for most women, though, whether pretty or plain."

"But how could she have divined that the key of the safe was in that drawer, or in that room?" urged Lennard. "For the matter of that, how could she have known that the will was in the safe?"

Truly the affair presented grave perplexities. "One curious part of it is that she should have called you up with her screams, Lennard," I remarked. "If she had only that moment opened the door, and seen—what frightened her, she could not have been already in the room hunting for the key. Were the screams assumed? Was it all a piece of acting?"

"It would take a subtle actress to counterfeit her terror," replied Lennard; "and the best actress breathing could not have assumed her ghastly look. No, Mr. Strange, I believe what she said was the fact: that, weary of waiting for her carriage, she had walked about the room, then opened the door, and passed into the other without any thought except that of distracting her ennui."

"She must have looked about for the key of the door, mind you, Lennard."

A man has rarely been placed in a more disagreeable predicament than I felt to be in then. It was of no use temporising with the matter: I could only meet it boldly, and I sent that evening for Sir Edmund Clavering, and laid it before him. I told him of Lady Clavering's visit, and hinted at the doubt which had forced itself on my mind. Sir Edmund jumped to the conclusion (and into a passion at the same time) that she was the culprit, and declared he would apply for a warrant at Bow Street on the morrow, to take her into custody. With extreme difficulty I got him to hear reason against anything of the sort.

Lennard, who had remained, came round to Sir Edmund's opinion that it must inevitably have been Lady Clavering. Failing her, no shadow of suspicion could attach itself to anyone, sift and search into the matter as we would.

"But neither was there as to the gold," was my rejoinder.

Then after they were gone, and I sat by the fire in the front room, and went over the details dispassionately and carefully, and lay awake the best part of the night, going over them still, my suspicions of Lady Clavering lessened, and I arrived at the conclusion that they were too improbable to be well founded.

Nevertheless, I intended to pursue the course I had decided on: and that was to call upon her. She, like Sir Edmund, was now staying in London, at an hotel. Not to accuse her, but to see if I could not, indirectly, make out something that would confirm or dissipate my suspicion.

I went up in the course of the morning. Lady Clavering was sitting alone, her widow's cap on the sofa beside her. She hurried it on to her head, when the waiter announced me.

"It is so hot and ugly," she exclaimed, in tones of excuse. "I sit without it when I am alone. So you have condescended to return my visit, Mr. Strange. I thought you gentlemen of the law took refuge in your plea of occupation to ignore etiquette."

"Indeed it is not out of deference to etiquette that I have called upon you to-day, Lady Clavering, but——"

"You have thought better of your refusal: you have come to say you will undertake my business!" she interrupted, eyes and looks full of eagerness.

"Nor yet that," I was forced to reply, though, in truth, I should have been glad to conciliate her. "I am sure you will find many an advocate quite as efficient as I should be. The day you were at our house, did you happen to see——"

"Mr. Strange, I must beg you, as a gentleman, not to allude to what I saw," she interposed, in tones of alarm. "I think it was inexcusable on your part not to have informed me what was in the next room."

"Pardon me, Lady Clavering; it would have been an unnecessary and unpleasant piece of information to volunteer: for how could I possibly foresee that you would be likely to enter that room?" I might have added—look for the key, unlock it, and go into it.

"I never saw a dead person in my life," she rejoined; "not even my husband; and I shall not easily recover from the shock. I would give anything rather than have been exposed to it."

"And so would I, and I shall always regret it," was my warm apology.

"Then why do you introduce the subject?"

"I did not intend to allude to that; but to your having sat in the front room I must allude; and I know you will excuse my asking you the question I am about to put to you. Did you happen to see a parchment lying in that front room: on the table, or the side-tables, or—anywhere, in short? We have missed one: and if you chanced to have noticed it, it would be a great assistance to us, as a proof that we need not carry our researches further back than that day."

"I don't remember that I saw any parchment," she carelessly rejoined. "I saw some papers, tied round with pink tape, on the table; I did not notice them particularly. I pray you not to make me think about that afternoon, or you will have me in hysterics again."

"It is not possible—your ladyship will pardon me—that it can have caught your dress in any way, and so have been carried downstairs and out of the house, and—perhaps—lost in the street?" I persisted slowly, looking at her.

Looking at her: but I could detect no emotion on her face; no drooping of the eye; no rise or fall of colour, such as one guilty would have been likely to display. She appeared to take my question literally, and to see nothing beyond it.

"I cannot tell anything about it, Mr. Strange. Had my dress been covered with parchments, I was in too much terror to notice them. Your clerks would be more able to answer you than I, for they had to assist me down to my carriage. But how should a parchment become attached to a lady's dress?" she added, shaking out the folds of her ample skirts. "The crape is quite soft, you perceive. Touch it."

"Quite so," I assented, advancing for a half-moment the extreme tip of my forefinger.

"You will take a glass of wine? Now don't say no. Why can't you be sociable?"

"Not any wine, thank you," I answered with a laugh. "We lawyers have to keep our heads clear, Lady Clavering: we should not do that if we took wine in the daytime."

"Sit still, pray. You have scarcely been here five minutes. I want to speak to you, too, upon a matter of business."

So I resumed my seat, and waited. She was looking at me very earnestly.

"It is about those missing letters of mine. Have you searched for them, Mr. Strange?"

"Partially. I do not think we hold any. There are none amongst the Clavering papers."

"Why do you say 'partially'?" she questioned.

"I have not had time to search amongst the packets of letters in Mr. Brightman's cupboards and places. But I think if there were any of your letters in our possession they would have been with the Clavering papers."

Her gaze again sought mine for a moment, and then faded to vacancy. "I wonder if he burnt them," she dreamily uttered.

"Who? Mr. Brightman?"

"No; my husband. You must look *everywhere*, Mr. Strange. If those letters are in existence, I must have them. You will look?"

"Certainly I will."

"I shall remain in town until I hear from you. You *will* go, then!"

"One more question ere I do go, Lady Clavering. Have you positively no recollection of seeing this lost parchment?"

She looked surprised at my pertinacity. "If I had, I should say so. I do not think I saw anything of the sort. But if I had seen it, the subsequent fright would have taken it clean out of my memory."

So I wished her good-morning and departed. "It is not Lady Clavering," I exclaimed to Lennard, when I reached home.

"Are you sure of that, Mr. Strange?"

"I think so. I judge by her manner: it is only consistent with perfect innocence. In truth, Lennard, I begin to see that I was foolish to have doubted her at all, the circumstances surrounding it are so intensely improbable."

And yet, even while I spoke, something of the suspicion crept into my mind again. So prone to inconsistency is the human heart.

CHAPTER VII.
ANNABEL.

MOST men have their romance in life sooner or later. Mine had come in due course, and she who made it for me was Annabel Brightman.

After my first meeting with her, when she was a child of fourteen, and I not much more than a lad of twenty, I had continued to see her from time to time, for Mr. Brightman's first invitation to me was only the prelude to others. I watched her grow up into a good, unaffected woman, lovable and charming as she was when a child. Childhood had passed away now, and thought and gentleness had taken its place; and to my eyes and my heart no other girl in the world could compare with Annabel Brightman.

Her father suspected it. Had he lived only a little longer, he would have learned it beyond doubt, for I should have spoken out more fully upon the matter.

A little less than a year before his death—it was on a Good Friday—I was spending the day at his house, and was in the garden with Annabel. She had taken my arm, and we were pacing the broad walk to the left of the lawn, thinking only of ourselves, when, raising my eyes, I saw Mr. Brightman looking attentively at us from one of the French windows. He beckoned to me, and I went in.

"Charles," said he, when I had stepped inside, "no *nonsense*. You and Annabel are too young for anything of that sort."

I felt that his eyes were full upon me as I stood before him, and my face flushed to the roots of my hair. But I took courage to ask a question.

"Sir, every year passing over our heads will lessen that objection. Would there be any other?"

"Be quiet, Charles. Time enough to talk of these things when the years shall have passed. You are too young for them, I say."

"I am twenty-five, sir; and Miss Brightman——"

"Twenty-five?" he interrupted. "I was past forty when I thought of marriage. You must not turn Annabel's head with visions of what the years may bring forth, for if you do I will not have you here. Leave that to the future."

But there was sufficient in Mr. Brightman's manner to prove that he had not been blind to the attachment springing up between us, and undoubtedly regarded me as the possible future husband of his daughter. At any rate he continued to invite me to his house. During the past year Annabel had been a great deal at Hastings with Miss Brightman; I wondered that her father and mother would spare her so much.

But Annabel knew nothing of that conversation, and I had never yet spoken of love to her. And now Mr. Brightman, who would, or at least might, have sanctioned it, was gone; and Mrs. Brightman, who would certainly, as I believed, oppose it, remained.

In the days immediately following Mr. Brightman's death, I was literally overwhelmed with business. Apart from the additional work that naturally fell upon me—his share as well as mine—no end of clients came pouring in; and for no earthly purpose, that I could see, excepting curiosity. Besides this, there was the frightful search for Sir Ralph Clavering's will, and the anxiety its loss entailed on me.

On the Wednesday afternoon, just as I had got rid of two clients, Lennard came up with the news that someone else was there. I was then in the front room, seated at Mr. Brightman's desk. Too impatient to hear Lennard out, I told him I could see no one; could not, and would not.

"It is Miss Annabel Brightman," rejoined Lennard quietly.

"Miss Annabel Brightman? Oh, that's very different; I will see her."

Annabel came in, throwing back her crape veil. She had driven up alone in the carriage to bring me a message from her mother. Mrs. Brightman had made an appointment with me for that evening at her house; she had now sent to tell me not to keep it, as she was not well enough to attend to business.

"Mamma wishes you to come to-morrow instead of to-day; early in the afternoon," added Annabel.

That would be impossible, and I said so; my engagements would not at present permit me to give up an afternoon.

"Perhaps to-morrow evening will do," I suggested. "In fact it must do, Annabel. I don't know when I shall have leisure to come down to you in the daytime."

"I dare say it will do," assented Annabel. "At any rate, you can come to us. If mamma is not able to enter into business matters, another time can be appointed."

"Is your mamma so very ill?"

"Sometimes I think so—but she fluctuates," replied Annabel. "She is extremely weak, and her spirits are depressed. She will pass whole hours shut up in her room in solitude. When I ask to go in, Hatch brings out a message that mamma is not able to see even me."

"Her illness must be on the nerves."

"I suppose so. Yesterday she came down and walked with me in the garden in the sunshine. She seemed pretty well then, but not strong. In the evening she shut herself up again."

"I wish you would sit down, Annabel," I said, offering her a chair for the third time.

"I would if I could stay. Mamma charged me to go straight back after leaving the message with you. Are you well?" she continued with hesitation. "You look harassed."

"I am well, Annabel. But you have used the right word—I am harassed; terribly so."

"Poor papa!" she sighed. "It has brought a world of work and care upon you, as well as of grief to us."

"I should not mind work. But—we have had another loss, Annabel. A loss as mysterious as that of the gold; and far more important."

"What is it?" she asked. "More money?"

"No; I wish it were. A will, deposited in the safe there, has disappeared. I cannot even guess at the consequences; ruin probably to me and to one of our best clients. Not only that. If things are to vanish so unaccountably from our strongholds, we must have an enemy at work, and it is impossible to foresee where it may end."

"How very strange! What was the will like? I mean, what did it look like? I have a reason for asking you."

"It was a folded parchment. You saw your father's will, Annabel: it looked very much like that. Why do you ask?"

"Because I remember papa's bringing home a parchment exactly like the one you describe. It was an evening or two before he died: the evening before I and mamma went to Hastings. We left on Saturday, so it must have been Friday. Do you think it could be the missing will?"

"Oh no. I have known Mr. Brightman—though very rarely—take home deeds which required studying; but he was not likely to take home Sir Ralph Clavering's will. He made it himself, and knew every word it contained. Annabel, I did not intend to let out the name, but it will be safe with you."

"Perfectly so; as safe as with yourself. I will not repeat it, even to mamma."

"And what I shall do I cannot tell," I concluded, as I attended her down to the carriage. "I would give every shilling I possess to find it."

More work, and then the afternoon came to an end, my dinner came up, and I was at liberty to enjoy a little rest. I had taken to the front room as my sitting-room, and should speedily remove the desk and iron safe into the other, making that exclusively a business-room, and seeing clients in it. After dinner, the fire clear, my reading-lamp lighted, I took up the newspaper. But for habits of order and self-denying rules, I should never have attained to the position I enjoyed. One of those rules was, never to read the *Times* or any work of relaxation until my work was over for the day. I could then enjoy my paper and my cigar, and feel that I had earned both.

I took up the *Times*, and almost the very first paragraph my eye fell upon was the following:

"We hear that the convict ship *Vengeance*, after encountering stormy weather and contrary winds on her passage out, has been wrecked upon an uninhabited island. It is said that some of the convicts have escaped."

I started up almost as if I had been shot. Tom Heriot had gone out in the *Vengeance*: was he one of those who had escaped? If so, where was he? and what would be his ultimate fate?

The ship had sailed from our shores in August; this was February: therefore the reader may think that the news had been long enough in reaching England. But it must be remembered that sailing-vessels were at the mercy of the winds and waves, and in those days telegrams and cablegrams had not been invented.

Throwing my cigar into the fire and the newspaper on the table, I fell into an unpleasant reverie. My lucky star did not seem in the ascendant just now. Mr. Brightman's unhappy death; this fresh uncertainty about Tom Heriot; the certain loss of the gold, and the disappearance of the will——

A ring at the visitors' bell aroused me. I listened, as Leah opened the door, curious to know who could be coming after office hours, unless it was Sir Edmund Clavering. Lake was in the country.

"Is Mr. Strange in, Leah?" And the sound of the sweet voice set my heart beating.

"Yes, Miss Brightman. Please go up."

A light foot on the stairs, and Annabel entered, holding up a parchment with its endorsement towards me. "Will of Sir Ralph Clavering."

"Oh, Annabel! you are my guardian angel!"

I seized the deed and her hands together. She smiled, and drew away the latter.

"I still thought the parchment I spoke of might be the missing one," she explained, "and when I got home I looked in papa's secretaire. There it was."

"And you have come back to bring it to me!"

"Of course I have. It would have been cruel to let you pass another night of suspense. I came as soon as I had dined."

"Who is with you?"

"No one; I came in by the omnibus. In two omnibuses really, for the first one only brought me as far as Charing Cross."

"You came in by omnibus! And alone?"

"Why not? Who was to know me, or what could harm me? I kept my veil down. I would not order the carriage out again. It might have disturbed mamma, and she is in bed with one of her worst headaches. And now, Charles, I must hasten back again."

"Wait one moment, Annabel, whilst I lock up this doubly-precious will."

"Why? You are not going to trouble yourself to accompany me, when you are so busy? It is not in the least necessary. I shall return home just as safely as I came here."

"You silly child! That you have come here at night and alone, I cannot help; but what would Mrs. Brightman say to me if I suffered you to go back in the same manner?"

"I suppose it was not quite right," she returned laughingly; "but I only thought of the pleasure of restoring the will."

I locked it up in the safe, and went downstairs with her. Why Mr. Brightman should have taken the will home puzzled me considerably; but the relief to my mind was inexpressible, and I felt quite a gush of remorse towards Lady Clavering for having unjustly suspected her.

The prosy old omnibus, as it sped on its way to Clapham, was to me as an Elysian chariot. And we had it to ourselves the whole way, but never a word passed between us that might not have been spoken before a committee of dowagers. In fact, we talked chiefly of Miss Brightman. I began it by asking how she was.

"Aunt Lucy is very delicate indeed," replied Annabel. "Papa's death has tried her greatly: and anything that tries her at once affects her chest. She says she shall not be able to risk another winter in England, even at Hastings."

"Where would she go?"

"To Madeira. At least, she thinks so now. In a letter mamma received from her yesterday, Aunt Lucy said she should go there in the autumn."

"She will find it very dull and lonely—all by herself."

"Yes," sighed Annabel. "Mamma said she should send me with her. But of course I could not go—and leave mamma. I wish I had a sister! One of us might then accompany Aunt Lucy, and the other remain at home. What do you think that stupid Hatch said?" cried Annabel, running on. "We were talking about it at lunch, and Hatch was in the room. 'It's just the best thing you can do, Miss Annabel, to go with your aunt,' she declared, following up mamma's remark."

"Perhaps Mrs. Brightman may take it into her head to go to Madeira also?"

Annabel made a movement of dissent. "No, I don't think she would do that, Charles. She and Aunt Lucy used to be the very best of friends, but lately there has been some coolness between them. The reason is not known to me, but I fancy Hatch knows it."

"Hatch seems to be quite a confidential attendant on your mamma."

"Oh yes, she is so. She has lived with us so long, you see; and mamma, when she was Miss Chantry, knew Hatch when she was quite a child. They both come from the same place—near Malvern, in Worcestershire. Aunt Lucy and mamma were intimate in early days, and it was through that intimacy that papa first knew Miss Chantry. Why she and Aunt Lucy should have grown cool to one another now, I cannot tell; but they have done so—and oh, I am sorry for it. I love Aunt Lucy very, very much," added the girl enthusiastically.

"And I'm sure I love the name—Lucy," I said, laughing. "It was my mother's."

The evening was yet early when we reached Mrs. Brightman's, for eight o'clock was striking. Hatch, in her new mourning, came stealing down the stairs with a quiet footfall, her black cap-strings flying as usual.

"Why, Miss Annabel, where have you been?" she cried. "I couldn't *imagine* what had become of you."

"I had to go out, Hatch—to take a deed to the office that poor papa had brought home and left here. Why? Has mamma wanted me?"

"Not she," returned Hatch. "She has just dropped off into a doze, and I am trying to keep the house free from noise. I thought you had been spirited away, Miss Annabel, and that's the truth."

"Mrs. Brightman has one of her bad headaches?" I remarked.

Hatch looked at me; then quickly at her young mistress: as much as to say: "You've been telling him that, Miss Annabel."

"It is that bad to-night, Mr. Charles, that her temples is fit to split," she answered. "Since master's death she have had 'em a'most constant—and no wonder, with all the worry and the shock it brought her. Are you going already, sir?"

"Will you not stay for tea?" asked Annabel.

"Not to-night, thank you," I replied.

"I'll let you out quietly," said Hatch, advancing towards the hall-door. "And mind, Miss Annabel, you are not to go anigh your mamma's room to waken her," she added, looking back dictatorially. "When one is racked with pain, body and mind, sleep is more precious than gold."

Hatch had lived there during the whole of Annabel's life, and could not always lay aside the authoritative manner she had exercised towards the child; possibly did not try to do so.

Great sway was held by Hatch in the household, and Mrs. Brightman appeared to sanction it. Certainly she never in any way interfered with it. But Hatch, always kindly, was a favourite with the servants.

With her shrewdness, capability and strong sense, it seemed a marvel that she should not have improved in manners and in her way of speaking. But she remained very much the same rough diamond that she had always been. Strangers were wont to feel surprise that Mrs. Brightman, herself so refined a woman, should put up with Hatch as her personal attendant; and in her attacks of illness Hatch would be in her mistress's room for hours together. At this time I knew nothing of Hatch's antecedents, very little of Mrs. Brightman's; or of matters relating to the past; and when circumstances brought me into Hatch's confidence, she enlightened me upon some points of the family history. A few of her communications I cannot do better than insert here, improving somewhat upon her parts of speech.

I recall the scene now. It was a lovely moonlit evening, not long after the time of which I am writing. I had gone to Clapham to inquire after Mrs. Brightman, who was then seriously ill, and kept her chamber. Strolling about the garden in the soft twilight, wishing Annabel was at home instead of at Hastings, Hatch came out and joined me, and at once fell to chatting without ceremony. I made a remark, quite by chance, that touched upon the subject of Mrs. Brightman's early life; it was immediately taken up by Hatch and enlarged upon. I heard much to which I had hitherto been a stranger.

"Colonel Chantry and his wife, who was the daughter of Lord Onyx, lived at their seat, Chantry Hall, a beautiful place not far from Malvern in Worcestershire. They had three children—George, Frederic and Emma, who were reared in all the pride and pomp of the Chantry family. The property was strictly entailed. It would descend to George Chantry at his father's death; and as Colonel Chantry had no other property whatever, and as he lived not only up to his income but beyond it, the future look-out for the younger son and the daughter was not a very great one.

"Such a dash they kept up," said Hatch, warming with her subject. "The Colonel liked show and parade, and Madam, as we always called her, had been born to it. She was the Honourable Mrs. Chantry, you see, sir, and chose to live according. They visited all the noble families round about, and were visited back again. The Somers' at Eastnor Castle, the Lyons' at Maddresfield, the Foleys at Whitley, the other Foleys at Stoke Edith, the Coventrys over at Croome, the Lechmeres at the Rhydd, the Hornyholds at Blacknore Park, and the Parkingtons at Ombersley—but there'd be no end if I stopped to tell you the half of 'em. Besides that, Mrs. Chantry counted a near relative in one of the cathedral prebendaries at Worcester—and for pride and exclusiveness some of those old prebendaries capped the world. So that——"

"But, Hatch, why are you telling me this?" I interrupted.

"To give you a notion of what my mistress was accustomed to when she was Miss Emma Chantry," promptly replied Hatch. "Well, Mr. Charles, they grew up, those three children, and I watched 'em grow; not that I was as old as they were; and I looked upon 'em as the finest and grandest young people in the world. The two sons spent a good deal more than they ought. Mr. Frederic especially, and the Colonel had to find a lot o' money, for 'twas wanted on all sides, and folks wondered how he did it. The end to it came all on a sudden—death."

"Whose death?"

"The Colonel's, sir. Mr. George, who was then Captain Chantry, and about twenty-seven years old, took the estate. But it was frightfully encumbered, and he complained bitterly to his mother that he should be a poor man for years and years to come. Madam resented what he said, and a quarrel ensued. She would not remain at the Hall, as he had expected her to do, but took a cottage at Malvern, and went into it with her daughter, with a parade of humility. She did not live very long after that, and Miss Emma was thrown on the world. Captain Chantry was married, then, to an earl's daughter; but his wife and Miss Emma did not get on together. Miss Emma refused to make her home at the Hall with Lady Grace, and she came to London on a visit to Miss Lucy Brightman, whose mother was living there. She and Miss Lucy had been at a finishing school together years before, and they had kept up their friendship. It was there she first saw Mr. Brightman, who was a great many years older than his sister; and it ended in their being married."

"And you came into their service, I suppose, Hatch?"

"I did, sir. They had been married near upon twelve months when young Mrs. Brightman found occasion to discharge two or three of her servants: and she wrote to the late housekeeper at Chantry Hall, asking her to find her some from our neighbourhood. London servants were *frightful*, she said: fine, lazy, extravagant and insolent. Mother heard about it, and spoke for me to go as under-housemaid. Well, I was engaged, Mr. Charles, and I came up here to Clapham: and I was called 'Hatch' from the beginning, because my Christian name, Emma, was the same as my lady's. Soon after this, Miss Annabel was born. It was my duty to wait upon the nurse and the sick-room; and my lady—who was ill and weakly for a long while—grew to like to have me there. She would talk about the old place to me, for you see I knew all the people in it as well as she did. Next, she made me upper-housemaid; and in a very few years, for she had found out how clever I was at dressmaking and with the needle generally, I became her maid."

"And you are in her confidence, Hatch?" I rejoined. "Deservedly so, I am sure."

"In a measure I am, Mr. Charles. A lady like my Missis, who never loses her pride day nor night, cannot descend to be over-confidential with an inferior. But I know she values me—and so did my poor master. I mayn't be polished, Mr. Charles, but I'd go through fire and water for them any day."

And I am sure she would have done so.

Well, this was a portion of what Hatch told me. But I must now go back to the night whose events were interrupted for the purpose of recording these details. Not that there is anything more to relate of the night in question. Leaving a message that I would call on Mrs. Brightman in good time the following evening, wishing Annabel good-night, and Hatch also, I returned home.

CHAPTER VIII.

PERRY'S REVELATION.

DEAR STRANGE,—Have you seen the news in to-day's paper? I have just caught sight of it. If the *Vengeance* has foundered, or whatever the mishap may be, and Tom Heriot should be one of the escaped prisoners, he will be sure to make his way home. Rely upon it he has not grown less reckless than he was, but probably has become more so. What trouble may not come of it? Do try and get at the particulars officially, as to whether there's truth in the report, or not; and let me know without delay.

Very truly yours,

Level.

Letters from Paris and the Continent generally were then usually delivered about mid-day. I was talking with Lennard in the front office when this one arrived. The clerks had gone to dinner.

"Have you heard the rumour about the ship *Vengeance*, Lennard?" I asked, laying down Lord Level's letter.

"I read it yesterday," he answered.

"I wonder how I could learn whether there's any foundation for it?"

Before he could answer me, we were interrupted by Major Carlen. He was in his usual state of excitement; his face lengthened, his arms thrown about, and his everlasting blue cloak trailing about him. I slipped the letter into my desk.

"Here's a pretty go, Charles!" he exclaimed. "Have you heard of it yet? That convict ship's gone to the bottom, and Tom Heriot has escaped."

"You should not assert that so positively, Major Carlen," I remonstrated. "It is not certain that any of the men have escaped, I suppose. If they have, Tom Heriot may not be one of them."

"But they have escaped," stuttered the gray old man, plumping himself down on a stool, around which his cloak fell like so much drapery. "Five have got off, and Tom is one of them."

"How do you know that?"

"How do I know it? How could I tell you if I didn't know it? Half an hour ago I met Percival in Downing Street, and he told me."

What little hope had been left within me took wings and flew away. Percival was First Lord of the Admiralty. He would certainly know the truth.

"Government has had official news of it," went on the Major gloomily; "and with it a list of the fugitives."

"And Tom's name is amongst them?"

"Tom's name is amongst them."

There was a pause. Lennard had gone into the other room. Major Carlen rose, saying something about lunch waiting for him at his club.

"Mark you, Charles: if Tom takes it into that rattle-pate of his to worm his way back to these shores, there may be the devil to pay. I hope with all my heart Level won't hear of this. The disgrace has been a precious thorn to him from the first."

"Blanche knows nothing at all of the matter as yet. She thinks Tom is with his regiment in India. The last time I saw her in Paris, not long before Mr. Brightman's death, she asked me what could be the reason Tom did not write to her."

"Much better tell her, and get it over," spoke the Major. "I should, if I were Level. He is more careful of her than she deserves—silly chit!"

Major Carlen and his cloak swung out again, the clerks came back, and the day and its duties went on. I wrote to Lord Level; giving him the substance of what the Major had heard, and telling him that I thought there could be little fear of Tom Heriot's venturing back to England. He could never be so reckless as to risk the danger.

Dinner over, I started for Mrs. Brightman's, and was admitted by the butler, who told me, in answer to my inquiry, that his mistress had been ill all day and had not come down. Tea waited on the drawing-room table, but no one was in the room. Presently Annabel entered.

"I am sorry you should have had the trouble to come, when perhaps you could not spare the time," she said. "Mamma is not well enough to see you."

"I was not busy to-night, Annabel. Perry has just told me your mamma has not been down to-day. Is her illness anything more than would be caused by these bad headaches? Do you fear anything serious?"

"Yes—no. I—I hope not."

Her voice and manner were excessively subdued, as if she could scarcely speak from fear of breaking down. She turned to the table, evidently to avoid my notice, and busied herself with the teacups.

"What is the matter, Annabel?"

"Nothing," she faintly answered, though her tears were even then falling. But I knew that some great trouble must be upon her.

"Is Mrs. Brightman vexed with you for having come up last night with that deed?"

"No; oh no! I told mamma about it this morning, and she said I had done quite right to take it up, but that I ought to have gone in the carriage."

"What, then, is causing you this grief?"

"You cannot expect me to be in very good spirits as yet," she replied: which was a decided evasion. "There are times—when I feel—the loss——"

She fairly broke down, and, sinking into a chair, cried bitterly and without concealment. I waited until she had become calmer.

"Annabel, my dear, sorrow for your loss is not all that disturbs your peace to-night. What else is there?"

"It is true that I have had something to vex me," she admitted after a pause. "But I cannot tell you about it."

"It is a momentary trouble, I hope; one that will pass away——"

"It will never pass away," she interrupted, with another burst of emotion. "It will be a weight and a grief upon me as long as life shall last. I almost wish I had died with my father, rather than have to live and bear it."

I took her hands in mine, and spoke deliberately. "If it be so serious a trouble as that, I must know it, Annabel."

"And if it were of a nature to be spoken of, you should know it. But it is not, and I can tell you nothing."

"Could you speak of it to your father, were he still living?"

"We should be compelled to speak of it, I fear. But——"

"Then, my dear, you can speak of it to me. From henceforth you must look upon me as in his place; your protector; your best friend: one who will share your cares, perhaps more closely than he could have done; who will strive to soothe them with a love that could not have been his. In a short time, Annabel, I shall ask you to give me the legal right to be and do this."

"It can never be," she replied, lifting her tearful eyes to mine.

I looked at her with an amused smile. I knew she loved me—and what other obstacle could exist? Mrs. Brightman might oppose it at first, but I did not despair of winning her over in the end.

"Not quite yet, I know," I answered her. "In a few months' time."

"Charles, you misunderstand me. I said it could never be. *Never.*"

"I certainly do not understand that. Had your father lived, it would have been; and I do not say this without reason for the assertion. I believe that he would have given you to me, Annabel, heartily, with all his good will."

"Yes, that may be true; I think you are right; but——"

"But what, then? One word, Annabel: the objection would not surely come from your heart?"

"No, it would not," she softly answered, blushing deeply. "Please do not speak of these things."

"I did not intend to speak of them so soon. But I wish to remind you that I do possess a right to share your troubles, of whatever nature those troubles may be. Come, my darling, tell me your grief."

"Indeed I cannot," she answered, "and you know I am not one to refuse anything from caprice. Let me go, Charles; I must make the tea."

I did let her go; but I bent over her first, without warning, and kissed her fervently.

"Oh, Charles!"

"As an earnest of a brother's love and care for you, Annabel, if you object for the present to the other," I whispered.

"Yes, yes; be a brother to me," she returned, with strange yearning. "No other tie can now be ours."

"My love, it *shall* be."

She rang for the urn, which Perry brought in, and then sat down to the table. I placed myself opposite to her and drew the dry toast towards me. "Mrs. Brightman prefers this, I believe; shall I prepare some for her?"

Annabel did not answer, and I looked up. She was struggling with her tears again. "I fear mamma is not well enough to eat," she said, in a stifled voice.

"Annabel!" I suddenly exclaimed, a light flashing upon me: "your mother is worse than you have confessed: it is her illness which is causing you this pain."

Far greater than any that had gone before was the storm of emotion that shook her now. I rose in consternation and approached her, and she buried her face in her hands. It was very singular. Annabel Brightman was calm, sensible, open as the day. She seemed to-night to have borrowed another character. Suddenly she rose, and nervously putting my hand aside, walked once or twice up and down the room, evidently to obtain calmness. Then she dried her eyes, and sat down again to the tea-tray. I confess that I looked on in amazement.

"Will you be kind enough to ring, Charles? Twice, please. It is for Hatch."

I did so, and returned to my seat. Hatch appeared in answer to her signal. Annabel held the cup of tea she had poured out.

"Mamma's tea, Hatch."

"She won't take none, miss."

It is impossible to resist the temptation of now and then giving the grammar and idioms Hatch had brought from her country home, and had never since attempted to alter or improve. But what Hatch lacked in accuracy she made up in fluency, for a greater talker never flourished under the sun.

"If you could get her to drink a cup, it might do her good," pursued Hatch's young mistress. "Take it up, and try."

Hatch flirted round, giving me full view of her black streamers, and brought forward a small silver waiter. "But 'twon't be of no manner of use, Miss Annabel."

"And here's some toast, Hatch," cried I.

"Toast, sir! Missis wouldn't look at it. I might as well offer her a piece of Ingy-rubbins to eat. Miss Annabel knows——"

"The tea will be cold, Hatch; take it at once," interposed Miss Annabel.

"Annabel, who is attending your mamma? Mr. Close, I suppose."

"Mr. Close. She never will have anyone else. I fear mamma must have been ill for some time; but I have been so much away with Aunt Lucy that I never noticed it before."

"Ay; Hastings and your aunt will miss you. I suppose Mrs. Brightman will not spare you now as she has hitherto done."

Annabel bent her head over the tea-tray, and a burning colour dyed her face. What had my words contained to call up the emotion? Presently she suddenly rose and left the room, saying she must see whether the tea had been taken. She returned with the empty cup, looking somewhat more cheerful.

"See, Charles, mamma *has* taken it: I do believe she would take more nourishment, if Hatch would only press it upon her. She is so very weak and depressed."

Annabel filled the cup again, and Hatch came in for it. "Suppose you were to take up a little toast as well; mamma might eat it," suggested Annabel, placing the cup on the waiter.

"Oh, well, not to contrairy you, Miss Annabel," returned Hatch. "I know what use it will be, though."

She held out the waiter, and I was putting the small plate of toast upon it, when screams arose from the floor above. Loud, piercing screams; screams of fear or terror; and I felt sure that they came from Mrs. Brightman. Hatch dropped the waiter on to the table, upsetting the tea, and dashed out of the room.

I thought nothing less than that Mrs. Brightman was on fire, and should have been upstairs as speedily as Hatch; but Annabel darted before me, closed the drawing-room door, and stood against it to prevent my exit, her arms clasping mine in the extremity of agitation, the shrieks above still sounding in our ears.

"Charles, you must not go! Charles, stay here! I ask it of you in my father's name."

"Annabel, are you in your senses? Your mother may be on fire! She must be on fire: do you not hear her screams?"

"No; it is nothing of that sort. I know what it is. You could do no good; only harm. I am in my own house—its mistress just now—and I tell you that you must not go up."

I looked down at Annabel. Her face was the hue of death, and though she shook from head to foot, her voice was painfully imperative. The screams died away.

A sound of servants was heard in the hall, and Annabel turned to open the door. "You will not take advantage of my being obliged to do so, Charles?" she hurriedly whispered. "You will not attempt to go up?"

She glided out and stood before the servants, arresting their progress as she had arrested mine. "It is only a similar attack to the one mamma had last night," she said, addressing them. "You know that it arises from nervousness, and your going up would only increase it. She prefers that Hatch alone should be with her; and if Hatch requires help, she will ring."

They moved away again slowly; and Annabel came back to the drawing-room.

"Charles," she said, "I am going upstairs. Pray continue your tea without waiting for me; I will return as soon as possible."

And all this time she was looking like a ghost and shaking like an aspen leaf.

I crossed to the fire almost in a dream and stood with my back to it. My eyes were on the tea-table, but they were eyes that saw not. All this seemed very strange. Something attracted my attention. It was the tea that Hatch had spilt, slowly filtering down to the carpet. I rang the bell to have it attended to.

Perry answered the ring. Seeing what was wrong, he brought a cloth and knelt down upon the carpet. I stood where I was, and looked on, my mind far away.

"Curious thing, sir, this illness of mistress's," he remarked.

"Is it?" I dreamily replied.

"The worst is, sir, I don't know how we shall pacify the maids," he continued. "I and Hatch both told them last night what stupids they were to take it up so, and that what missis saw could not affect them. But now that she has seen it a second time—and of course there was no mistaking the screams just now—they are turning rebellious over it. The cook's the most senseless old thing in the world! She vows she won't sleep in the house to-night; and if she carries out her threat, sir, and goes away, she'll spread it all over the neighbourhood."

Was Perry talking Sanscrit? It was about as intelligible to me as though he had been. He was still over the carpet, and in matter-of-fact tones which shook with his exertion, for he was a fat man, and was rubbing vehemently, he continued:

"I'm sure I couldn't have believed it. I wouldn't have believed it, sir, but that I have been in the house and a witness to it, as one may say; at any rate, heard the screams. For a more quieter, amiabler, and peaceabler man never lived than my master, kind to all about him, and doing no harm to anybody; and why he should 'Walk' is beyond our comprehension."

"Why he should--what?" I exclaimed.

"Walk, sir," repeated Perry. "Hatch says it's no doubt on account of his dying a sudden death; that he must have left something untold, and won't be laid till he has told it. It's apparent, I take it, that it concerns Mrs. Brightman, by his appearing to her."

"What is it that has appeared to Mrs. Brightman?" I asked, doubting my ears.

Perry arrested his occupation, and raised himself to look at me. "My dead master, sir," he whispered mysteriously. "Master's ghost."

"Your master's—ghost!" I echoed.

"Yes, sir. But I thought my young lady had told you."

I felt an irreverent inclination to laugh, in spite of the serious surroundings of the topic. Ghosts and I had never had any affinity with each other. I had refused to believe in them as a child, and most unhesitatingly did so as a man. When I returned "The Old English Baron" to Annabel, some years before, she wished she had never lent it to me, because I declined to accept the ghost.

"I am sure, sir, I never supposed but what Miss Annabel must have imparted it to you," repeated Perry, as if doubting his own discretion in having done so. "But somebody ought to know it, if it's only to advise; and who so fit as you, sir, master's friend and partner? *I* should send for a clergyman, and let him try to lay it; that's what I should do."

"Perry, my good man," and I looked at his bald head and rotund form, "you are too old, and I should have thought too sensible, to believe in ghosts. How can you possibly listen for a moment to stories so absurd as these?"

"Well, sir," argued Perry, "my mistress did see it or she didn't; and if she didn't, why should she scream and say she did? You heard her screams just now; and they were worse yesterday."

"Did you see the ghost?"

"No, sir; I was not up there. Hatch thought she saw it as she went into the room. It was in a corner, and wore its shroud: but when we got up there it was gone."

"When was all this?"

"Last night, sir. When you left, Miss Annabel took off her bonnet in the drawing-room and rang for tea, which I carried in. Presently Hatch ran in at the front door, and Miss Annabel told me to call her in. 'Has mamma had her tea, Hatch?' said my young lady. 'Yes, she has,' returned Hatch; which was a downright falsehood, for she had not had any. But Hatch is master and missis too, as far as we servants go, and nobody dares contradict her. Perhaps she only said it to keep Mrs. Brightman undisturbed, for she knows her ailments and her wants and ways better than Miss Annabel. So, sir, I went down, and Hatch went up, but not, it seems, into Mrs.

Brightman's room, for she thought she was asleep. In two or three minutes, sir, the most frightful shrieks echoed through the house; those to-night were nothing half as bad. Hatch was first in the chamber, Miss Annabel next, and we servants last. My mistress stood at the foot of the bed, which she must have left————"

"Was she dressed?" I interrupted.

"No, sir; she was in her night-gown, or a dressing-gown it might have been. She looked like—like—I don't hardly know what to say she looked like, Mr. Strange, but as one might suppose anybody would look who had seen a ghost. She was not a bit like herself. Her eyes were starting and her face was red with terror; almost all alight, as one may say; indeed, she looked mad. As to her precise words, sir, I can't tell you what they were, for when we gathered that it was master's ghost which she had seen, appearing in its shroud in the corner by the wardrobe, the women servants set up a cry and ran away. That stupid cook went into hysterics, and declared she wouldn't stop another night in the house."

"What was done with Mrs. Brightman?"

"Miss Annabel—she seemed terrified out of her senses, too, poor young lady—bade me hasten for Mr. Close; but Hatch put in her word and stopped me, and said the first thing to be done was to get those shrieking maids downstairs. Before I and John had well done it—and you'd never have forgot it, sir, had you seen 'em hanging on to our coat tails—Hatch followed us down, bringing her mistress's orders that Mr. Close was not to be fetched; and indeed, as Hatch remarked, of what use could a doctor be in a ghost affair? But this morning Miss Annabel sent for him."

"Mrs. Brightman must have had a dream, Perry."

"Well, sir, I don't know; it might have been; but she is not one given to dreams and fancies. And she must have had the same dream again now."

"Not unlikely. But there's no ghost, Perry; take my word for it."

"I hope it will be found so, sir," returned Perry, shaking his head as he retired; for he had done his work and had no further pretext for lingering.

CHAPTER IX.
SOMEONE ELSE SEEN.

STANDING with my back to the fire in the drawing-room, waiting for Annabel's return, the tea growing cold on the table, I puzzled over what I had just heard, and could make nothing of it. That Mr. Brightman's spirit should appear to his wife seemed to be utterly incomprehensible; was, of course, incredible. That many people believed in the reappearance of the dead, I well knew; but I had not yet made up my mind to become one of them.

It was inexplicable that a woman in this enlightened age, moving in Mrs. Brightman's station, could yield to so strange a delusion. But, allowing that she had done so, did this sufficiently explain Annabel's deep-seated grief? or the remark that her grief would end only with her life? or the hint that she could never be my wife? And why should she refuse to confide these facts to me? why, indeed, have prevented my going upstairs? I might have reassured Mrs. Brightman far more effectually than Hatch; who, by Perry's account, was one of the believers in the ghost theory. It was altogether past comprehension, and I was trying hard to arrive at a solution when Hatch came in, her idioms in full play.

"My young lady's complemens, sir, and will you excuse her coming down again to-night? she is not equal to seeing nobody. And she says truth, poor child," added Hatch, "for she's quite done over."

"How is your mistress now, Hatch?"

"Oh, she's better, she is. Her nerves have been shook, sir, of late, you know, through the shock of master's unexpected death, and in course she starts at shadders. I won't leave the room again, without the gas a-burning full on."

"What is this tale about Mr. Brightman?"

Hatch and her streamers swung round, and she closed the door before answering. "Miss Annabel never told you *that*; did she, sir?"

"No; but I have heard a word or two elsewhere. You fancy you saw a ghost?"

"Missis do."

"Oh, I thought you did also."

"I just believe it's a delusion of hers, Mr. Charles, and nothing more," returned Hatch confidently. "If master had been a bad sort of character, or had taken his own life, or anything of that, why, the likelihood is that he might have walked, dying sudden. But being what he was, a Christian gentleman that never missed church, and said his own prayers at home on his knees regular—which I see him a doing of once, when I went bolt into his dressing-room, not beknowing he was in it—why, it is not likely, sir, that he comes again. I don't say as much to them downstairs; better let them be frightened at his ghost than at—at—anybody else's. I wish it was master's ghost, and nothing worse," abruptly concluded Hatch.

"Nothing worse! Some of you would think that bad enough, were it possible for it to appear."

"Yes, sir, ghosts is bad enough, no doubt. But realities is worse."

So it was of no use waiting. I finished my cup of cold tea, and turned to go, telling Hatch that I would come again the following evening to see how things were progressing.

"Yes, do, Mr. Charles; you had better," assented Hatch, who had a habit, not arising from want of respect, but from her long and confidential services, and the plenitude of her attachment, of identifying herself with the family in the most unceremonious manner. "Miss Annabel's life hasn't been a bed of roses since this ghost appeared, and I fear it is not likely to be, and if there's anybody that can say a word to comfort her, it must be you, sir; for in course I've not had my eyes quite blinded. Eyes is eyes, sir, and has their sight in 'em, and we can't always shut 'em, if we would."

Hatch was crossing the hall to open the door for me, and I had taken my great-coat from the stand, when Annabel flew down the stairs, her face white, her voice sharp with terror.

"Hatch! Hatch! mamma is frightened again!"

Hatch ran up, two stairs at a time, and I went after her. Mrs. Brightman had followed Annabel, and now stood outside her chamber-door in her white dressing-gown, trembling violently. "He is watching me again," she panted: "he stands there in his grave-clothes!"

"Don't you come," cried Hatch, putting Annabel back unceremoniously. "I shall get my missis round best alone; I'm not afraid of no ghostesses, not I. Give a look to her, sir," she added, pointing to Annabel, as she drew Mrs. Brightman into her chamber, and fastened the door.

Annabel, her hands clasped on her chest, shook as she stood. I put my arm round her waist and took her down to the drawing-room. I closed the door, and Annabel sat down on the sofa near the fire.

"My darling, how can I comfort you?"

A burst of grief prevented her from replying—grief that I had rarely witnessed. I let it spend itself; you can do nothing else with emotion so violent: and when it was over I sat down beside her.

"Annabel, you might have confided this to me at first. It can be nothing but a temporary delusion of Mrs. Brightman's, arising from a relaxed state of the nervous system. Imaginary spectral appearances——"

"Who told you about that?" she interrupted, in agitation. "How came you to hear it?"

"My dear, I heard it from Perry. But he did not break faith in speaking of it, for he thought you had already told me. There can be no reason why I should not know it; but I am sorry that it has penetrated to the servants."

Poor Annabel laid her head on the arm of the sofa, and moaned.

"I do not like to leave you or Mrs. Brightman either, in this distress. Shall I remain in the house to-night? I can send a message to Leah——"

"Oh no, no," she hastily interrupted, as if the proposal had startled her. And then she continued slowly, hesitatingly, pausing between her words: "You do not—of course—believe that—that papa——"

"Of course I do not," was my hearty reply, relieving her from her embarrassing question. "Nor you either, Annabel: although, as a child, you devoured every ghost-story you came near."

She made no confirmatory reply, only looked down, and kept silence. I gazed at her wonderingly.

"It terrified me so much last night," she whispered.

"What terrified you, Annabel?"

"I was terrified altogether; at mamma's screams, at her words, at the nervous state she was in. Mr. Close has helped to frighten me, too, for I heard him say this morning to Hatch that such cases have been known to end in madness."

"Mr. Close is not worth a rush," cried I, suppressing what I had been about to utter impulsively. "So he knows of this fancy?"

"Yes, Hatch told him. Indeed, Charles, I do not see that there was any help for it."

"He will observe discretion, I suppose. Still, I almost wish you had called in someone who is a stranger to the neighbourhood."

"Mamma will not have a stranger, and you know we must not act in opposition to her will. She seemed so much better this morning; quite herself again."

"Of course. With the return of daylight these fancies subside. But as it seems there is nothing I can do for you, Annabel, I must be going, and will come again to-morrow evening."

The conclusion seemed to startle her. "Had—you—better come?" she cried, with much hesitation.

"Yes, Annabel, I had better come," I firmly replied. "And I cannot understand why you should wish me not to do so, as I can see you do."

"Only—if mamma should be ill again—it is all so uncomfortable. I dare say you never even finished your tea," glancing at the table. All trivial excuses, to conceal her real and inexplicable motive, I felt certain. "Good-night, Charles."

She held out her hand to me. I did not take it: I took her instead, and held her to my heart. "You are not yourself to-night, Annabel, for there is some further mystery in all this, and you will not tell it me. But the time will soon come, my dearest, when our mysteries and our sorrows must be shared in common." And all the answer I received was a look of despair.

In passing through the iron gates, I met Mr. Close. The moon to-night was obscured by clouds, but the gas-lamps revealed us plainly to each other. "How is Mrs. Brightman?" he asked.

"Very ill and very strange," I answered. "Do you apprehend any serious result?"

"Well—no," said he; "not immediately. Of course, it will tell upon her in the long-run."

"She has had another attack of nervous terror to-night; in fact, two attacks."

"Ay; seen the ghost again, I suppose. I suspected she would, so thought I would just call in."

"Would it not be as well—excuse me, Mr. Close, but you are aware how intimately connected I was with Mr. Brightman—to call in a consultation? Not that there is the slightest doubt of your skill and competency, but it appears to be so singular a malady; and in the multitude of counsellors there is safety, you know."

"It is the commonest malady we have to deal with," returned he; and the answer was so unexpected that I could only stare in silence.

"Have a consultation if you think it more satisfactory, Mr. Strange. But it will not produce the slightest benefit; and the less this matter is allowed to transpire the better. I assure you that all the faculty combined could not do more for Mrs. Brightman than I am doing. It is a lamentable disease, but it is one that must run its course."

He went on to the house, and I got outside an omnibus that was passing the end of the road, and lighted my cigar, more at sea than ever. If seeing ghosts was the commonest malady doctors had to deal with, where had I lived all my life not to have learned it?

The next afternoon I was surprised by a visit from Perry. He brought word from his mistress that she was very much better, though not yet able to see me on business matters; when she felt equal to it, she would let me know. Miss Annabel, concluded the butler, was gone to Hastings.

"To Hastings!" I exclaimed.

"Well, yes, sir. My mistress decided upon it this morning, and I have just seen her off by train, with Sarah in attendance on her. Fact is, sir," added Perry, dropping his voice to a confidential key: "Hatch whispered to me that it was thought best the poor young lady should be out of the house while it is so troubled."

"Troubled!" I repeated, half in scorn.

"Why, yes, sir, you know what it is that's in it," rejoined Perry simply. "Mr. Close, too, he said Miss Annabel ought to be away from it just now."

When every hour of the day is occupied, time glides on insensibly. A week passed. I heard no news of or from Mrs. Brightman, and did not altogether care to intrude upon her, unbidden. But when the second week was also quickly passing, I determined to take an evening to go to Clapham. Dinner over, I was going downstairs, and met Leah coming up.

"If anyone calls, I am out for the evening, Leah," I said to her. "And tell Watts when he comes in that I have left the *Law Times* on the table for Mr. Lake. He must take it round to him."

"Very well, sir."

I was nearing the top of Essex Street when I met the postman.

"Anything for me?" I inquired, for I had expected an important letter all day.

"I think there is, sir," he replied, looking over his letters under the gas-lamp. "'Messrs. Brightman and Strange;' there it is, sir."

I opened it by the same light. It was the expected letter, and required an immediate answer. So I returned, and letting myself in with my latch-key, went into the front office to write it.

Leah had not heard me come in. She was upstairs, deep in one of the two favourite ballads which now appeared to comprise all her collection. During office hours Leah was quiet as a mute; but in the evening she would generally croon over one of these old songs in an undertone, if she thought that I was out and she had the house to herself. As she was thinking now, for she sang out in full key, but in a doleful, monotonous sort of chant. Her voice was still very sweet, but had lost much of the power of its earlier days. One of these two songs was a Scotch fragment, beginning "Woe's me, for my heart is breaking;" the other was "Barbara Allen." Fragmentary also, apparently; for as Leah sang it there appeared to be neither beginning nor ending to it.

"And as she wandered up and down,
She heard the bells a-ringing,
And as they rang they seemed to say,
'Hard-hearted Barbara Allen.'

"She turned her body round and round,
She saw his corpse a-coming;
'Oh, put him down by this blade's side,
That I may gaze upon him!'

"The more she looked, the more she laughed,
The further she went from him;
Her friends they all cried out, 'For shame,
Hard-hearted Barbara Allen!'"

Whether this is the correct version of the ballad or not, I do not know; it was Leah's version. Many and many a time had I heard it; and I was hearing it again this evening, when there came a quiet ring at the door bell. My door was pushed to but not closed, and Leah came bustling down. Barbara Allen was going on still, but in a more subdued voice.

"Do Mr. Strange live here?" was asked, when the door was opened.

"Yes, he does," responded Leah. "He is out."

"Oh, I don't want him, ma'am. I only wanted to know if he lived here. What sort of a man is he?"

"What sort of a man?" repeated Leah. "A very nice man."

"Yes; but in looks, I mean."

"Well, he is very good-looking. Blue eyes, and dark hair, and straight features. Why do you want to know?"

"Ay, that's him. But I don't know about the colour of his eyes; I thought they was dark. Blue in one light and brown in another, maybe. A tallish, thinnish man."

"He's pretty tall; not what can be called a maypole. A little taller than Mr. Brightman was."

"Brightman and Strange, that's it? T'other's an old gent, I suppose?" was the next remark; while I sat, amused at the colloquy.

"He was not old. He is just dead. Have you any message?"

"No, I don't want to leave a message; that's not my business. He told me he lived here, and I came to make sure of it. A pleasant, sociable man, ain't he; no pride about him, though he is well off and goes cruising about in his own yacht."

"No pride at all with those he knows, whether it's friends or servants," returned Leah, forgetting her own pride, or at any rate her discretion, in singing my praises. "Never was anybody pleasanter than he. But as to a yacht——"

"Needn't say any more, ma'am; it's the same man. Takes a short pipe and a social dram occasionally, and makes no bones over it."

"What?" retorted Leah indignantly. "Mr. Strange doesn't take drams or smoke short pipes. If he just lights a cigar at night, when business is over, it's as much as he does. He's a gentleman."

"Ah," returned the visitor, his tones expressing a patronizing sort of contempt for Leah's belief in Mr. Strange: "gents that is gents indoors be not always gents out. Though I don't see why a man need be reproached with not being a gent because he smokes a honest clay pipe, and takes a drop short; and Mr. Strange does both, I can tell ye."

"Then I know he does not," repeated Leah. "And if you knew Mr. Strange, you wouldn't say it."

"If I knew Mr. Strange! Perhaps I know him as well as you do, ma'am. He don't come courting our Betsy without my knowing of him."

"What do you say he does?" demanded Leah, suppressing her wrath.

"Why, I say he comes after our Betsy; leastways, I'm a'most sure of it. And that's why I wanted to know whether this was his house or not, for I'm not a-going to have her trifled with. She's my only daughter, and as good as he is. And now that I've got my information I'll say good-night, ma'am."

Leah shut the door, and I opened mine. "Who was that, Leah?"

"My patience, Mr. Charles!" she exclaimed in astonishment. "I thought you were out, sir."

"I came in again. Who was that man at the door?"

"Who's to know, sir—and what does it matter?" cried Leah. "Some half-tipsy fellow who must have mistaken the house."

"He did not speak as though he were tipsy at all."

"You must have heard what he said, sir."

"I heard."

Leah turned away, but came back hesitatingly, a wistful expression in her eyes. I believe she looked upon me as a boy still, and cared for me as she did when I had been one. "It is not true, Mr. Charles?"

"Of course it is not true, Leah. I neither take drams short, nor go courting Miss Betsys."

"Why, no, sir, of course not. I believe I must be getting old and foolish, Mr. Charles. I should just like to wring that man's neck for his impudence!" she concluded, as she went upstairs again.

But what struck me was this: either that one of my clerks was playing pranks in my name—passing himself off as Mr. Strange, to appear great and consequential; and if so, I should uncommonly like to know which of them it was—or else that something was being enacted by those people who made the sorrow of Leah's life; that daughter of hers and the husband—as we will call him. For the voice at the door had sounded honest and the application genuine.

Posting my letter, I made the best of my way to Clapham. But I had my journey for nothing, and saw only Perry. His mistress had been getting much better, he said, but a day or two ago she had a relapse and was again confined to her room, unable to see anyone. Mr. Close had ordered her to be kept perfectly quiet. Annabel remained at Hastings.

"And what about that fright, Perry, that you were all so scared with a fortnight ago?" I asked, as he strolled by my side back to the iron gates: for it was useless for me to go in if I could not see Mrs. Brightman. "Has the house got over it yet?"

"Sir, it is in the house still," he gravely answered.

"Do you mean the scare?"

"I mean the ghost, sir. Poor master's spirit."

I turned to look at his face, plainly enough to be discerned in the dimness of the foggy night. It was no less grave than his words had been.

"The figure does not appear every night, sir; only occasionally," he resumed; "and always in the same place—in the corner by the wardrobe in Mrs. Brightman's bedroom. It stands there in its grave-clothes."

What with the dark trees about us, the weird evening, and Perry's shrinking tones, I slightly shivered, for all my unbelief.

"But, Perry, it is *impossible*, you know. There must be delusion somewhere. Mrs. Brightman's nerves have been unstrung by her husband's death."

"Hatch has seen it twice, Mr. Strange," he rejoined. "Nobody can suspect Hatch of having nerves. The last time was on Sunday night. It stood in its shroud, gazing at them—her and the mistress—with a mournful face. Master's very own face, sir, Hatch says, just as it used to be in life; only white and ghastly."

It was a ghastly subject, and the words haunted me all the way back to town. Once or twice I could have declared that I saw Mr. Brightman's face, pale and wan, gazing at me through the fog. Certainly Hatch had neither nerves nor fancies; no living woman within my circle of acquaintance possessed less. What did it all mean? Where could the mystery lie?

Stirring the fire into a blaze when I got into my room, I sat before it, and tried to think out the problem. But the more I tried, the more effectually it seemed to elude me.

With the whir-r-r that it always made, the clock on the mantelpiece began to strike ten. I started. At the same moment, the door opened slowly and noiselessly, and Leah glided in. Mysteriously, if I may so express it: my chamber candlestick carried in one hand, her shoes in the other. She was barefooted; and, unless I strangely mistook, her face was as ghastly as the one Perry had been speaking of that night.

Putting the candlestick on a side-table, slipping her feet into her shoes, and softly closing the door, she turned to me. Her lips trembled, her hands worked nervously; she seemed unable to speak.

"Why, Leah!" I exclaimed, "what is the matter?"

"Sir," she then said, in the deepest agitation; "I have seen to-night that which has almost frightened me to death. I don't know how to tell you about it. Watts has dropped asleep in his chair in the kitchen, and I took the opportunity to steal up here. I wouldn't let him hear it for the world. He is growing suspicious, fancying I'm a bit odd at times. He'd be true in this, I know, but it may be as well to keep it from him."

"But what is it, Leah?"

"When I saw him, I thought I should have dropped down dead," she went on, paying no attention to the question. "He stood there with just the same smile on his face that it used to wear. It was *himself*, sir; it was, indeed."

May I be forgiven for the folly that flashed over me. Occupied as my mind was with the apparition haunting the house at Clapham, what could I think but that Leah must have seen the same?

"You mean Mr. Brightman," I whispered.

"Good heavens!" she exclaimed, approaching nearer to me, whilst glancing over her shoulder as if in dread that the ghost were following her: "does *he* come again, Mr. Charles? Have you seen him? Is he in the house?"

"No, no; but I thought you meant that, Leah. Who is it that you have seen?"

"Mr. Tom, sir. Captain Heriot."

CHAPTER X.
PROWLING ABOUT.

SO the blow had fallen. What we were dreading had come to pass. Tom Heriot was back again.

I sat half-paralyzed with terror. Leah stood before me on the hearthrug, pouring out her unwelcome disclosure with eager words now that her first emotion had subsided. She went on with her tale more coherently, but in undertones.

"After you had gone out this evening, Mr. Charles, I was in the kitchen, when one of those small handfuls of gravel I dread to hear rattled against the window. 'Nancy,' I groaned, my heart failing me. I could not go to the door, lest Watts should come up and see me, for I expected him back every minute; and, sure enough, just then I heard his ring. I gave him the *Law Times*, as you bade me, sir, telling him he was to take it round to Mr. Lake at once. When he was gone I ran up to the door and looked about, and saw Nancy in the shadow of the opposite house, where she mostly stands when waiting for me. I could not speak to her then, but told her I would try and come out presently. Her eldest boy, strolling away with others at play, had been run over by a cab somewhere in Lambeth; he was thought to be dying; and Nancy had come begging and praying me with tears to go with her to see him."

"And you went, I suppose, Leah. Go on."

"You know her dreadful life, Mr. Charles, its sorrows and its misery; how could I find it in my heart to deny her? When Watts came back from Mr. Lake's, I had my bonnet and shawl on. 'What, going out?' said he, in surprise, and rather crossly—for I had promised him a game at cribbage. 'Well,' I answered, 'I've just remembered that I have to fetch those curtains home to-night that went to be dyed; and I must hasten or the shop may be shut up. I've put your supper ready in case they keep me waiting, but I dare say I shall not be long.'"

To attempt to hurry Leah through her stories when once she had entered upon them, was simply waste of words; so I listened with all the patience I had at command.

"The boy had been carried into a house down Lambeth way, and the doctor said he must not be moved; but the damage was not as bad, sir, as was at first thought, and I cheered Nancy up a bit by saying he would get all right and well. I think he will. Leaving her with the lad, I was coming back alone, when I missed my way. The streets are puzzling just there, and I am not familiar with them. I thought I'd ask at a book-stall, and went towards it. A sailor was standing outside, fingering the books and talking to somebody inside that I couldn't see. Mr. Charles, I had got within a yard of him, when I saw who it was—and the fright turned me sick and faint."

"You mean the sailor?"

"Yes, sir, the sailor. It was Captain Heriot, disguised. Oh, sir, what is to be done? The boy that I have often nursed upon my knee—what will become of him if he should be recognised?"

The very thought almost turned me sick and faint also, as Leah expressed it. How could Tom be so foolhardy? An escaped convict, openly walking about the streets of London!

"Did he see you, Leah?"

"No, sir; I stole away quickly; and the next turning brought me into the right road again."

"How did he look?"

"I saw no change in him, sir. He wore a round glazed hat, and rough blue clothes, with a large sailor collar, open at the throat. His face was not hidden at all. It used to be clean-shaved, you know, except the whiskers; but now the whiskers are gone, and he wears a beard. That's all the difference I could see in him."

Could this possibly be Tom? I scarcely thought so; scarcely thought that even he would be as reckless of consequences.

"Ah, Mr. Charles, do you suppose I could be mistaken in him?" cried Leah, in answer to my doubt. "Indeed, sir, it was Captain Heriot. He and the man inside—the master of the shop, I suppose—seemed talking as if they knew one another, so Mr. Tom may have been there before. Perhaps he is hiding in the neighbourhood."

"Hiding!" I repeated, in pain.

"Well, sir——"

"Leah! have you gone up to bed?"

The words came floating up the staircase in Watts's deep voice. Leah hurried to the door.

"I came up to bring the master's candle," she called out, as she went down. "If you hadn't gone to sleep, you might have heard him ring for it."

All night I lay awake, tormented on the score of Tom Heriot. Now looking at the worst side of things, now trying to see them at their best, the hours dragged along, one after the other, until daybreak. In spite of Leah's statement and her own certainty in the matter, my mind refused to believe that the sailor she had seen could be Tom. Tom was inconceivably daring; but not daring enough for this. He would have put on a more complete disguise. At least, I thought so.

But if indeed it was Tom—why, then there was no hope. He would inevitably be recaptured. And this meant I knew not what of heavier punishment for himself; and for the rest of us further exposure, reflected disgrace, and mental pain.

Resolving to go myself at night and reconnoitre, I turned to my day's work. In the course of the morning a somewhat curious thing happened. The old saying says that "In looking for one thing you find another," and it was exemplified in the present instance. I was searching Mr. Brightman's small desk for a paper that I thought might be there, and, as I suppose, accidentally touched a spring, for the lower part of the desk suddenly loosened, and I found it had a false bottom to it. Lifting the upper portion, I found several small deeds of importance, letters and other papers; and lying on the top of all was a small packet, inscribed "Lady Clavering," in Mr. Brightman's writing.

No doubt the letters she was uneasy about, and which I had hitherto failed to find. But now, what was I to do? Give them back to her? Well, no, I thought not. At any rate, not until I had glanced over them. Their being in this secret division proved the importance attaching to them.

Untying the narrow pink ribbon that held them together, there fell out a note of Sir Ralph Clavering's, addressed to Mr. Brightman. It was dated just before his death, and ran as follows:

> "I send you the letters I told you I had discovered. Read them, and keep them safely. Should trouble arise with her after my death, confront her with them. Use your own discretion about showing them or not to my nephew Edmund. But should she acquiesce in the just will I have made, and when all things are settled on a sure foundation, then destroy the letters, unseen by any eye save your own; I do not wish to expose her needlessly.—R. C."

Lady Clavering had not acquiesced in the will, and she was still going on with her threatened and most foolish action. I examined the letters. Some were written *to* her; not by her husband, though; some were written *by* her:

and, take them for all in all, they were about as damaging a series as any it was ever my fate to see.

"The senseless things these women are!" thought I. "How on earth came she to preserve such letters as these?"

I sent a messenger for Sir Edmund Clavering. Mr. Brightman was to use his own discretion: I hardly thought any was left to me. It was more Sir Edmund's place to see them than mine. He came at once.

"By George!" he exclaimed, when he had read two or three of them, his handsome face flushing, his brow knit in condemnation. "What a despicable woman! We have the cause in our own hands now."

"Yes; she cannot attempt to carry it further."

We consulted a little as to the best means of making the truth known to Lady Clavering—an unthankful office that would fall to me—and Sir Edmund rose to leave.

"Keep the letters safely," he said; almost in the very words Sir Ralph had written. "Do not bring them within a mile of her hands: copies, if she pleases, as many as she likes. And when things are upon a safe footing, as my uncle says, and there's no longer anything to fear from her, then they can be destroyed."

"Yes. Of course, Sir Edmund," I continued, in some hesitation, "she must be spared to the world. This discovery must be held sacred between us——"

"Do you mean that as a caution?" he interrupted in surprise. "Why, Strange, what do you take me for?"

He clasped my hand with a half-laugh, and went out. Yes, Lady Clavering had contrived to damage herself, but it would never transpire to her friends or her enemies.

Leah had noticed the name of the street containing the book-stall, and when night came I put on a discarded old great-coat and slouching hat, and set out for it. It was soon found: a narrow, well-frequented street, leading out of the main thoroughfare, full of poor shops, patronized by still poorer customers.

The book-stall was on the right, about half-way down the street. Numbers of old books lay upon a board outside, lighted by a flaring, smoking tin lamp. Inside the shop they seemed chiefly to deal in tobacco and snuff. Every now and then the master of the shop—whose name, according to the announcement above the shop, must be Caleb Lee—came to the door to look about him, or to answer the questions of some outside customer touching the books. But as yet I saw no sign of Tom Heriot.

Opposite the shop, on the other side the way, was a dark entry; into that entry I ensconced myself to watch.

Tired of this at last, I marched to the end of the street, crossed over, strolled back on the other side the way, and halted at the book-stall. There I began to turn the books about: anything to while away the time.

"Looking for any book in particular, sir?"

I turned sharply at the question, which came from the man Lee. The voice sounded familiar to my ear. Where had I heard it?

"You have not an old copy of the 'Vicar of Wakefield,' I suppose?"—the work flashing into my mind by chance.

"No, sir. I had one, but it was bought last week. There's 'Fatherless Fanny,' sir; that's a very nice book; it was thought a deal of some years ago. And there's the 'Water Witch,' by Cooper. That's good, too."

I remembered the voice now. It was that of Leah's mysterious visitor of the night before, who had been curiously inquisitive about me. Recognition came upon me with a shock, and opened up a new fear.

Taking the "Water Witch"—for which I paid fourpence—I walked on again. Could it be possible that *Tom Heriot* was passing himself off for me? Why, this would be the veriest folly of all. But no; that was altogether impossible.

Anxious and uneasy, I turned about again and again. The matter ought to be set at rest, yet I knew not how to do it.

I entered the shop, which contained two small counters: the one covered with papers, the other with smoking gear. Lee stood behind the former, serving a customer, who was inquiring for last week's number of the *Fireside Friend*. Behind the other counter sat a young girl, pretty and modest. I turned to her.

"Will you give me a packet of bird's-eye?"

"Yes, sir," she answered in pleasant tones; and, opening a drawer, handed me the tobacco, ready wrapped up. It would do for Watts. Bird's-eye, I knew, was his favourite mixture.

"Thank you, sir," she said, returning me the change out of a florin. "Anything else, sir?"

"Yes; a box of wax matches."

But the matches were not to be found, and the girl appealed to her father.

"Wax matches," returned the man from across the shop. "Why, they are on the shelf behind you, Betsy."

The matches were found, the girl took the money for them, and thanked me again. All very properly and modestly. The girl was evidently as modest and well-behaved as a girl could be.

So that was Betsy! But who was it that was courting her in my name? One of my office clerks—or Captain Thomas Heriot?

Captain Thomas Heriot did not make his appearance, and I began to hope that Leah had been mistaken. It grew late. I was heartily tired, and turned to make my way home.

Why I should have looked round I cannot tell, but I did look round just as I reached the end of the street. Looming slowly up in the distance was a sailor, with a sailor's swaying walk, and he turned into the shop.

I turned back also, all my pulses quickened. I did not follow him in, for we might have betrayed ourselves. I stood outside, occupied with the old books again, and pulled the collar of my coat well up, and my hat well down. Not here must there be any mutual recognition.

How long did he mean to stay there? For ever? He and Lee seemed to be at the back of the shop, talking together. I could not hear the voices sufficiently to judge whether one of them was that of Tom Heriot.

He was coming now! Out he came, puffing at a fresh-lighted pipe, his glazed hat at the back of his head, his face lifted to the world.

"Tell you we shall, master. Fine to-morrow? not a bit of it. Rain as sure as a gun. This dampness in the air is a safe sign on't. Let a sailor alone for knowing the weather."

"At sea, maybe," retorted Caleb Lee. "But I never yet knew a sailor who wasn't wrong about the weather on shore. Good-night, sir."

"Good-night to you, master," responded the sailor.

He lounged slowly away. It was not Tom Heriot. About his build and his fair complexion, but shorter than Tom. A real, genuine Jack-tar, this, unmistakably. Was he the man Leah had seen? This one wore no beard, but bushy, drooping whiskers.

"Looking for another book, sir?"

In momentary confusion, I caught up the book nearest to hand. It proved to be "Fatherless Fanny," and I said I'd take it. While searching for the money, I remarked that the sailor, just gone away, had said we should have rain to-morrow.

"I don't see that he is obliged to be right, though he was so positive over it," returned the man. "I hate a rainy day: spoils our custom. Thankye, sir. Sixpence this time. That's right."

"Do many sailors frequent this neighbourhood?"

"Not many; we've a sprinkling of 'em sometimes. They come over here from the Kent Road way."

Well, and what else could I ask? Nothing. And just then a voice came from the shop.

"Father," called out Miss Betsy, "is it not time to shut up?"

"What do you ask? Getting a little deaf, sir, in my old age. Coming, Betsy."

He turned into the shop, and I walked away for the night: hoping, ah! how earnestly, that Leah had been mistaken.

"Mr. Strange, my lord."

It was the following evening. Restlessly anxious about Tom Heriot, I betook myself to Gloucester Place as soon as dinner was over, to ask Major Carlen whether he had learnt anything further. The disreputable old man was in some way intimate with one or two members of the Government. To my surprise, Sanders, Lord Level's servant, opened the door to me, and showed me to the dining-room. Lord Level sat there alone over his after-dinner claret.

"You look as if you hardly believed your eyes, Charles," he laughed as he shook hands. "Sit down. Glasses, Sanders."

"And surprised I may well look to see you here, when I thought you were in Paris," was my answer.

"We came over to-day; got here an hour ago. Blanche was very ill in crossing and has gone to bed."

"Where is Major Carlen?"

"Oh, he is off to Jersey to see his sister, Mrs. Guy. At least, that is what he said; but he is not famous for veracity, you know, and it is just as likely that he may be catching the mail train at London Bridge *en route* for Homburg, as the Southampton train from Waterloo. Had you been half an hour earlier, you might have had the pleasure of assisting at his departure. I have taken this house for a month, and paid him in advance," added Lord Level, as much as to say that the Major was not altogether out of funds.

A short silence ensued. The thoughts of both of us were no doubt busy. Level, his head bent, was slowly turning his wine-glass round by its stem.

"Charles," he suddenly said, in a half-whisper, "what of Tom Heriot?"

I hardly knew how to take the question.

"I know nothing more of him," was my answer.

"Is he in London, think you? Have you heard news of him, in any way?"

Now I could not say that I had heard news: for Leah's information was not news, if (as I hoped) she was mistaken. And I judged it better not to speak of it to Lord Level until the question was set at rest. Why torment him needlessly?

"I wrote you word what Major Carlen said: that Tom was one of those who escaped. The ship was wrecked upon an uninhabited island, believed to be that of Tristan d'Acunha. After a few days some of the convicts contrived to steal a boat and make good their escape. Of course they were in hope of being picked up by some homeward-bound ship, and may already have reached England."

"Look here," said Lord Level, after a pause: "that island lies, no doubt, in the track of ships bound to the colonies, but not in the track of those homeward-bound. So the probability is, that if the convicts were sighted and picked up, they would be carried further from England, not brought back to it."

I confess that this view had not occurred to me; in fact, I knew very little about navigation, or the courses taken by ships. It served to strengthen my impression that Leah had been in error.

"Are you sure of that?" I asked him.

"Sure of what?" returned Lord Level.

"That the island would be out of the track of homeward-bound vessels."

"Quite sure. Homeward-bound vessels come round Cape Horn. Those bound for the colonies go by way of the Cape of Good Hope."

"My visit here to-night was to ask Major Carlen whether he had heard any further particulars."

"I think he heard a few more to-day," said Lord Level. "The *Vengeance* was wrecked, it seems, on this island. It is often sighted by ships going to the colonies, and the captain was in hope that his signals from the island would be seen, and some ship would bear down to them. In vain. After the convicts—five of them, I believe—had made their escape, he determined to send off the long-boat, in charge of the chief officer, to the nearest Australian coast, for assistance. On the 10th of December the boat set sail, and on Christmas Day was picked up by the *Vernon*, which reached Melbourne the last day of the year."

"But how do you know all these details?" I interrupted in surprise.

"They have been furnished to the Government, and Carlen was informed of them this morning," replied Lord Level. "On the following day, the 1st of January, the ship *Lightning* sailed from Melbourne for England; she was furnished with a full account of the wreck of the *Vengeance* and what succeeded to it. The *Lightning* made a good passage home, and on her arrival laid her reports before the Government. That's how it is."

"And what of the escaped convicts?"

"Nothing is known of them. The probability is that they were picked up by an outward-bound ship and landed in one of the colonies. If not, they must have perished at sea."

"And if they were so picked up and landed, I suppose they would have reached England by this time?"

"Certainly—seeing that the *Lightning* has arrived. And the convicts had some days' start of the long-boat. I hope Tom Heriot will not make his way here!" fervently spoke Lord Level. "The consequences would three-parts kill my wife. No chance of keeping it from her in such a hullabaloo as would attend his recapture."

"I cannot think how you have managed to keep it from her as it is."

"Well, I have been watchful and cautious—and we have not mixed much with the gossiping English. What! are you going, Charles?"

"Yes, I have an engagement," I answered, as we both rose. "Good-night. Give my love to Blanche. Tell her that Charley will see her to-morrow if he can squeeze out a minute's leisure for it."

Taking up the old coat I had left in the passage, I went out with it on my arm, hailed a cab that was crossing Portman Square and was driven to Lambeth. There I recommenced my watch upon the book-stall and the street containing it, not, however, disclosing myself to Lee that night. But nothing was to be seen of Tom Heriot.

CHAPTER XI.
MRS. BRIGHTMAN.

SUR this coms hoppin youle excuse blundurs bein no skollerd sur missis is worse and if youle com ive got som things to tell you I darnt keep um any longer your unbil servint emma hatch but doant say to peri as i sent."

This remarkable missive was delivered to me by the late afternoon post. The schoolmaster must have been abroad when Hatch received her education.

I had intended to spend the evening with Blanche. It was the day subsequent to her arrival from France with Lord Level, and I had not yet seen her. But this appeared to be something like an imperative summons, and I resolved to attend to it.

"The more haste, the less speed." The proverb exemplifies itself very frequently in real life. Ordering my dinner to be served half an hour earlier than usual, I had no sooner eaten it than a gentleman called and detained me. It was close upon eight o'clock when I reached Clapham.

Perry, the butler, received me as usual. "Oh, sir, such a house of sickness as it is!" he exclaimed, leading the way to the drawing-room. "My mistress is in bed with brain-fever. They were afraid of it yesterday, but it has quite shown itself to-day. And Miss Annabel is still at Hastings. I say she ought to be sent for; Hatch says not, and tells me to mind my own business: but——"

Hatch herself interrupted the sentence. She came into the room and ordered Perry out of it. The servants, even Perry, had grown into the habit of obeying her. Closing the door, she advanced to me as I stood warming my hands at the fire, for it was a sharp night.

"Mr. Strange, sir," she began in a low tone, "did you get that epistle from me?"

I nodded.

"You've not been down here much lately, sir. Last night I thought you might come, the night afore I thought it. The last time you did come you never stepped inside the door."

"Where is the use of coming, Hatch, when I am always told that Mrs. Brightman cannot see me—and that Miss Annabel remains at Hastings?"

"And a good thing that she do remain there," returned Hatch. "Perry, the gaby, says, 'Send for Miss Annabel: why don't you write for Miss Annabel?' But that his brains is no bigger than one o' them she-gooses' on Newland Common, he'd have found out why afore now. Sir," continued Hatch, changing her tone, "I want to know what I be to do. I'm not a person of edication or book-learning, but my wits is alive, and they serves me instead. For this two or three days past, sir, I've been thinking that I ought to tell out to somebody responsible what it is that's the matter with my missis, and I know of nobody nearer the family than you, sir. There's her brother, in course, at the Hall, Captain Chantrey, but my missis has held herself aloof from him and Lady Grace, and I know she'd be in a fine way if I spoke to him. Three or four days ago I said to myself, 'The first time I see Mr. Strange, I'll tell him the truth.' Last night she was worse than she has been at all, quite raving. I got frightened, which is a complaint I'm not given to, and resolved not to let another day pass, and then, whether she lived or died, the responsibility would not lie upon my back."

Straightening myself, I stood gazing at Hatch. She had spoken rapidly. If I had caught all the words, I did not catch their meaning.

"Yes?" I said mechanically.

"And so, with morning light, sir, I wrote you that epistle."

"Yes, yes; never mind all that. What about Mrs. Brightman?"

Hatch dropped her voice to a lower and more mysterious whisper. "Sir, my missis gives way, she do."

"Gives way," I repeated, gazing at Hatch, and still unable to see any meaning in the words. "What do you say she does?"

Hatch took a step forward, which brought her on the hearthrug, close to me. "Yes, sir; missis gives way."

"Gives way to what?" I reiterated. "To her superstitious fancies?"

"No, sir, to stimilinks."

"To——" The meaning, in spite of Hatch's obscure English, dawned upon me now. A cold shiver ran through me. Annabel's mother! and honoured Henry Brightman's wife!

"She takes stimulants!" I gasped.

"Yes, sir; stimilinks," proceeded Hatch. "A'most any sort that comes anigh her. She likes wine and brandy best; but failing them, she'll drink others."

Question upon question rose to my mind. Had it been known to Mr. Brightman? Had it been a prolonged habit? Was it deeply indulged in? But Annabel was her child, and my lips refused to utter them.

"It has been the very plague of my life and my master's to keep it private these many months past," continued Hatch. "'Hatch does this in the house, and Hatch does the other,' the servants cry. Yes; but my master knew why I set up my authority; and missis knew it too. It was to screen her."

"How could she have fallen into the habit?"

"It has grown upon her by degrees, sir. A little at first, and a little, and then a little more. As long as master was here, she was kept tolerably in check, but since his death there has been nobody to restrain her, except me. Whole days she has been in her room, shutting out Miss Annabel, under the excuse of headaches or lowness, drinking all the time; and me there to keep the door. I'm sure the black stories I have gone and invented, to pacify Miss Annabel and put her off the right scent, would drive a parson to his prayers."

"Then Miss Annabel does not know it?"

"She do now," returned Hatch. "The first night there was that disturbance in the house about missis seeing the ghost, her room was thrown open in the fright, and all the house got in. I turned the servants out: I dared not turn out Miss Annabel, and she couldn't fail to see that her mother was the worse for drink. So then I told her some, and Mr. Close told her more next morning."

Annabel's strange grief, so mysterious to me, was accounted for now. Hatch continued:

"You see now, sir, why Miss Annabel has been kept so much at Hastings. Master would never have her at home for long together, afeared her mother might betray herself. He wanted to keep the child in ignorance of it, as long as it was possible. Miss Brightman knew it. She found it out the last time she was visiting here; and she begged my missis on her bended knees to be true to herself and leave it off. Missis promised—and such a bout of crying they two had together afore Miss Lucy went away! For a time she did get better; but it all came back again. And then came master's death—and the shock and grief of that has made her give way more than she ever did. And there it is, sir. The secret's got too weighty for me; I couldn't keep it to myself any longer."

"Perry says Mrs. Brightman is now lying ill with brain-fever."

"We call it brain-fever to the servants, me and Mr. Close; it's near enough for them," was Hatch's cool reply. "The curious thing is that Perry don't seem to suspect; he sees more of his missis than the rest do, and many a time must have noticed her shaking. Last night her fit of shaking was dreadful—and her fever too, for the matter of that. She is as close as she well can be upon that disorder that comes of drink. If it goes on to a climax, nothing can save the disgrace from coming out downstairs."

Nothing could or would save it, in my opinion, downstairs or up, indoors or out. What a calamity!

"But she is a trifle better to-night," continued Hatch. "The medicines have taken effect at last, and put her into a deep sleep, or else I couldn't be talking here."

"Did you invent the episode of Mr. Brightman's ghost, Hatch, by way of accounting for Mrs. Brightman's state to the servants?" I inquired.

"*I* invent it!" returned Hatch. "I didn't invent it. My missis did see it. Not, I take it, that there was any ghost to see, in one sense; but when these poor creatures is in the shakes, they fancy they see all kinds of things—monkeys and demons, and such-like. I can't believe it was master. I don't see why he should come back, being a good man; and good men that die in peace be pretty sure to rest in their graves. Still, I'd not be too sure. It may be that he comes back, as my missis fancies, to silently reproach her. It's odd that she always sees him in the same place, and in his shroud. Several times she has seen him now, and her description of how he looks never varies. Nothing will ever persuade her, sick or well, that it is fancy."

"You have seen him also, I hear?"

"Not I," said Hatch. "I have upheld what my missis says. For which was best, Mr. Strange, sir—to let the servants think she is shaking and raving from fear of a ghost, or to let 'em get to suspect her the worse for drink?"

Hatch's policy had no doubt been wise in this. I told her so.

"I have seen the shakes before to-day; was used to 'em when a child, as may be said," resumed Hatch. "I had a step-uncle, sir, mother's half-brother, who lived next door to us; he was give to drink, and he had 'em now and then. Beer were his chief weakness; wine is missis's. If that step-uncle of mine had been put to stand head downwards in a beer barrel, Mr. Charles, he'd not have thought he had enough. He'd be always seeing things, he would; blue and red and green imps that crawled up his bed-posts, and horrid little black devils. He used to start out of doors and run away for fear of 'em. Once he ran out stark naked, all but his shoes; he tore past the cottages all down the village, and flung himself into the pond opposite the stocks. All the women watching him from their doors and windows followed after him. The men thought it were at least a mad dog broke loose, seeing the women in pursuit like that; whereas it were nothing but my step-uncle in one of his bouts—stripped. Mrs. Brightman would never do such a thing as that, being a lady; but they be all pretty much alike for sense when the fit is on 'em."

"And Mr. Brightman knew of this, you say? Knew that she was given to—to like stimulants?"

"He couldn't be off knowing of it, sir, habiting, as he did, the same rooms: and it has just bittered his life out. She has never had a downright bad attack, like this one, therefore we could hide it from the servants and from Miss Annabel, but it couldn't be hided from him. He first spoke to me about it six or seven months ago, when he was having an iron bedstead put up in the little room close to hers; until then he had made believe to me not to see it. Sometimes I know he talked to her, all lovingly and persuasively, and I would see her with red eyes afterwards. I once heard her say, 'I will try, Henry; indeed I will;' and I do believe she did. But she got worse, and then master spoke to Mr. Close."

"Has it been long growing upon her?" I asked, in a low voice.

"Sir," returned Hatch, looking at me with her powerful eyes, "it has been growing for years and years. I think it came on, first, from idleness——"

"From idleness!"

"I mean what I say, sir. She married master for a home, as it were, and she didn't care for him. She cared for somebody else—but things wouldn't work convenient, and they had to part. Miss Emma Chantrey was high-born and beautiful, but she had no money, and the gentleman had no money either, so it would not do. It was all over and done with long before she knew Mr. Brightman. Well, sir, she married and come home here. But she never liked the place; commercial, she said, these neighbourhoods was, round London, and the people were beneath her. So she wouldn't visit, and she wouldn't sew nor read; she'd just sit all day long with her hands afore her, a-doing of nothing. I saw that as soon as I took service here. 'Wait,' said I to myself, 'till the baby comes.' Well, it came, sweet little Miss Annabel, but it didn't make a pin's difference: missis got a maid for it, and then a governess, and turned her over to them. No more babies followed; pity but what a score of 'em had; they might have roused her from her apathy."

"But surely she did not give way, as you call it, then?"

"No, not then. She was just ate up with weariness; she found no pleasure in life, and she did no work in it; when morning broke she'd wish the day was over; and when night came she'd wish it was morning; and so the years went by. Then she got to say—it come on quite imperceptible—'Hatch, get me a glass of wine; I'm so low and exhausted.' And I used to get her one, thinking nothing. She took it then, just because she wanted something to rouse her, and didn't know what. That was the beginning of it, Mr. Charles."

"A very unfortunate beginning."

"But," continued Hatch, "after a while, she got to like the wine, and in course o' time she couldn't do without it; a glass now and a glass then between her meals, besides what she took with them, and it was a great deal; pretty nigh a bottle a-day I fancy, altogether. Master couldn't make out how it was his wine went, and he spoke sharp to Perry; and when missis found that, she took to have some in on her own account, unbeknowing to him. Then it grew to brandy. Upon the slightest excuse, just a stitch in her side, or her finger aching, she would say, 'Hatch, I must have half a glass of hot brandy-and-water.' Folks don't stop at the first liquor, sir, when it gets to that pitch; my step-uncle would have swallowed vitriol sooner than have kept to beer."

"Hatch, this is a painful tale."

"And I've not finished of it," was Hatch's response. "Missis had an illness a year or eighteen months back; I dare say you remember it, sir. Weak enough she was when she began to get about; some people thought she wouldn't live. 'She must take stimilinks to strengthen her,' says Close. 'She don't want stimilinks,' says I; 'she'll get better without 'em;' for she was a taking of 'em then in secret, though he didn't know it. 'Mrs. Brightman must take stimilinks,' says he to master. 'Whatever you thinks necessary,' returns master—though if he hadn't begun to suspect then, it's odd to me. And my missis was not backward to take Close's stimilinks, and she took her own as well; and that I look upon as the true foundation of it all; it might never have grown into a habit but for that; and since then matters have been going from bad to worse. It's a dangerous plan for doctors to order stimilinks to weak people," added Hatch reflectively; "evil comes of it sometimes."

I had heard that opinion before; more than once. I had heard Mr. Brightman express it to a client, who was recovering from an illness. Was he thinking of his wife?

"And for the last six months or so my missis has been getting almost beyond control," resumed Hatch; "one could hardly keep her within bounds. Me and master tried everything. We got Miss Annabel out of the way, not letting her come home but for two or three days at a time, and them days—my patience! if I hadn't to watch missis like a cat! She didn't wish to exceed in the daytime when Miss Annabel was here, though she would at night; but you know, sir, these poor creatures can't keep their resolves; and if she once got a glass early, then all her prudence went to the winds. I did my best; master did his best; and she'd listen, and be reasonable, and say she'd touch nothing. But upon the least temptation she'd give way. My belief is, she couldn't help it; when it comes to this stage it's just a disease. A disease, Mr. Charles, like the measles or the yellow jaundice, and they can't put it from 'em if they would."

True.

"On the Thursday night, it was the Thursday before the master died, there was a quarrel," Hatch went on. "Mrs. Brightman was not fit to appear at the dinner-table, and her dinner was sent up to her room, and master came upstairs afterwards, and they had words. Master said he should send Miss Annabel to Hastings in the morning and keep her there, for it would be impossible to hide matters from her longer if she stayed at home. Mrs. Brightman, who was not very bad, resented that, and called him harsh names: generally speaking, she was as humble as could be, knowing herself in the wrong and feeling ashamed of it. They parted in anger. Master was as good as his word; he sent Miss Annabel with Sarah down to Hastings on the Friday morning to Miss Brightman. In the evening, when he came home to dinner, missis was again the worse for drink. But on the Saturday morning she was up betimes, afore the household even, and had ordered the carriage, and went whirling off with me to the station to take the first train for Hastings. 'I shall return on Monday and bring back Annabel,' she said to master, when she was stepping into the carriage at the door, and he ran out to ask where she was going, for he had not seen nor heard nothing about it. 'Very well,' said he in a whisper; 'only come back as you ought to come.' Mr. Charles, I think those were the only words that passed between them after the quarrel."

"You mean the quarrel on the Thursday night?"

"Yes, sir; there was no other quarrel. We went to the Queen's Hotel. And on the Sunday, if you remember, you came down to tell us of the master's sudden death. Mrs. Brightman was ill that morning, really ill, I mean, with one of her dreadful headaches—which she did have at times, and when she didn't they was uncommon convenient things for me to fall back upon if I needed an excuse for her. She had meant to go to church, but was not able. She had had too much on the Saturday night, though she was always more prudent out than at home, and was worried in mind besides. But, to be sure, how she did take on about master's death when alone with me. They had parted bad friends: leastways had not made it up after the quarrel; she knew how aggravating she had been to him in it, and a notion got hold of her that he might have poisoned himself. When she learnt the rights of it, that he had died peaceful and natural, she didn't get much happier. She was perpetually saying to me, as the days went on, that her conduct had made him miserable. She drank then to drown care; she fancied she saw all sorts of things, and when it came to master's ghost——"

"She could not have been sober when she fancied that."

"Nor was she," returned Hatch. "Half-and-half like; had enough to betray herself to Miss Annabel. 'Now don't you go and contradict about the ghost,' I says to her, poor child; 'better let the kitchen think it's a ghost than brandy-and-water.' Frightful vexed and ashamed missis was, when she grew sober, to find that Miss Annabel knew the truth. She told her she must go to her aunt at Hastings for a time: Mr. Close, he said the same. Miss Annabel would not go; she said it was not right that she should leave her mother, and there was a scene; miss sobbing and crying, mistress angry and commanding; but it ended in her going. 'I don't want no spies upon me,' says missis to me, 'and she shall stop at Hastings for good.' Since then she has been giving way unbearable, and the end of it is, she has got the shakes."

What a life! What a life it had been for Mr. Brightman! Lennard had thought of late that he appeared as a man who bore about him some hidden grief! Once, when he had seemed low-spirited, I asked whether anything was amiss. "We all have our trials, Charles; some more, some less," was the answer, in tones that rather shut me up.

Hatch would fain have talked until now: if wine was her mistress's weakness, talking was hers; but she was interrupted by the arrival of Mr. Close, and had to attend him upstairs. On his return he came into the drawing-room.

"This is a disagreeable business, Mr. Strange. Hatch tells me she has informed you of the true nature of the case."

A disagreeable business! The light words, the matter-of-fact tone seemed as a mockery. The business nearly overwhelmed *me*.

"When you met me the other night, at the gate, and spoke of Mrs. Brightman's illness, I was uncertain how to answer you," continued Mr. Close. "I thought it probable you might be behind the curtain, connected as you are with the family, but I was not sure."

"I never had the faintest suspicion of such a thing, until Hatch's communication to me to-night. She says her young mistress, even, did not know of it."

"No; they have contrived to keep it from Annabel."

"Will Mrs. Brightman recover?"

"From this illness? oh dear yes! She is already in a fair way for it, having dropped into the needed sleep; which is all we want. If you mean will she recover from the habit—why, I cannot answer you. It has obtained a safe hold upon her."

"What is to be done?"

"What can be done?" returned the surgeon. "Mrs. Brightman is her own mistress, subject to no control, and has a good income at command. She may go on drinking to the end."

Go on drinking to the end! What a fearful thought! what a fearful life! Could *nothing* be done to prevent it; to recall her to herself; to her responsibility for this world and the next?

"I have seen much of these cases," continued Mr. Close; "few medical men more. Before I came into this practice I was assistant-surgeon to one of the debtors' prisons up in town: no school equal to that in all Europe for initiating a man into the mysteries of the disorder."

"Ay, so I believe. But can Mrs. Brightman's case be like those cases?"

"Why should it differ from them? The same habits have induced it. Of course, she is not yet as bad as some of them are, but unless she pulls up she will become so. Her great chance, her one chance, I may say, would be to place herself under some proper control. But this would require firm resolution and self-denial. To begin with, she would have to leave her home."

"This cannot be a desirable home for Annabel."

"No. Were she my child, she should not return to it."

"What is to be done when she recovers from this attack?"

"In what way?"

In what way, truly! My brain was at work over the difficulties of the future. Was Mrs. Brightman to live on in this, her home, amidst her household of curious servants, amidst the prying neighbours, all of whom would revel in a tale of scandal?

"When she is sufficiently well she should have change of air," proceeded the doctor, "and get her nerves braced up. Otherwise she may be seeing that ghost for six months to come. A strange fancy that, for her to take up—and yet, perhaps, not so very strange, taking all things into consideration. She is full of remorse, thinking she might have done her duty better by her husband, made him less unhappy, and all that. Mrs.

Brightman is a gentlewoman of proud, elevated instincts: she would be only too thankful to leave off this demoralizing habit; in a way, I believe she strives to do it, but it is stronger than she is."

"It has become worse, Hatch says, since Mr. Brightman died."

"Undoubtedly," concluded Mr. Close. "She had taken it to drown care."

CHAPTER XII.
MY LORD AND MY LADY.

THE breakfast-table was laid in Gloucester Place, waiting for Lord and Lady Level. It was the day following the one recorded in the last chapter. A clear, bright morning, the sun shining hotly.

Blanche came in, wearing a dainty white dress. Her face, though thin, was fair and lovely as ever; her eyes were as blue and brilliant. Ringing for the coffee to be brought in, she began turning over the letters on the table: one for herself, which she saw was from Mrs. Guy; three for her husband. Of these, one bore the Paris postmark.

"Here is a letter from Paris, Archibald," she said to him as he entered. "I think from Madame Sauvage; it is like her writing. I hope it is to say that she has sent off the box."

"That you may regain possession of your finery," rejoined Lord Level, with a light, pleasant laugh. "Eh, Blanche?"

"Well, my new lace mantle is in it. So stupid of Timms to have made the mistake!"

"So it was. I dare say the box is on its road by this time."

Blanche began to pour out the coffee. Lord Level had gone to the window, and was looking up and down the street. As he took his seat to begin breakfast, he pushed the letters away idly without opening them, and remarked upon the fineness of the morning.

They were fairly good friends, these two; always courteous, save when Blanche was seized with a fit of jealousy, persuading herself, rightly or wrongly, that she had cause for it. Then she would be cross, bitter, snappish. Once in a way Lord Level retorted in kind; though on the whole he was patient and gentle with her. In the midst of it all she loved him passionately at heart, and sometimes let him know it.

"As it is so fine a day, Archibald, you might take me to Kensington, to call on Mrs. Page Reid, this afternoon. She sent us her address, you know."

"I would rather not, Blanche, unless you particularly wish it. I don't care to keep up Mrs. Page Reid's acquaintance. She's good for nothing but to talk scandal."

"I do not much care for her either," acknowledged Blanche. "We are not in the least obliged to renew her acquaintance."

"I will take you somewhere else instead," said he, pleased at her acquiescence. "We will go out after luncheon and make an afternoon of it—like Darby and Joan."

Presently, when breakfast was nearly over, Blanche opened her letter from Mrs. Guy; reading out scraps of it to her husband. It told of Major Carlen's arrival—so that he had really gone to Jersey. Then she took up the *Times*. An unusual thing for her to do. She did not care for newspapers, and Lord Level did not have them sent to him when in Paris: he saw the English journals at the club. No doubt he had his reasons for so doing.

Meanwhile he was opening his own letters. The one from Paris came last. Had his wife been looking at him, she might have seen a sudden change pass over his face as he read it, as though startled by some doubt or perplexity.

"Archibald, what can this mean?" exclaimed Blanche in breathless tones. "Listen: 'The names of the five convicts said to have escaped from the ship *Vengeance* after her wreck on the island, supposed to be that of Tristan d'Acunha, are the following: George Ford, Walter Green, John Andison, Nathaniel Markham, and Thomas Heriot.' That is Tom's name."

Cramming all his letters into his breastpocket with a hurried movement, Lord Level quietly took the paper from his wife's hands. This was the very contretemps he had so long striven to guard against.

"My dear Blanche, do you suppose there is only one Thomas Heriot in the world?" cried he carelessly. "'Ship *Vengeance*?' 'Escape of convicts?' Oh, it is something that has happened over at Botany Bay."

"Well, the name startled me, at the moment. I'm sure Tom might as well be a convict as anything else for all the news he sends us of himself."

"He was always careless, you know, and detested letter-writing."

Carrying away the paper, Lord Level left the room and went to the one behind it, of which he made a sort of study. There he sat down, spread the letter from Paris before him on the table, and reperused it.

"Confound the woman!" remarked his lordship. "I shall have to go down there now!"

Breakfast removed, Blanche began at once to write to Mrs. Guy, whose letter required an answer. That over, she put on her bonnet to call on Mrs. Arnold Ravensworth in Langham Place. She had called on the previous day, but found Mr. and Mrs. Ravensworth out of town: they were expected home that evening. So now Blanche went again.

Yes, they had arrived; and had brought with them Blanche's old friend, Cecilia Ravensworth, from White Littleham Rectory.

How happy they were together, these two! It seemed an age since they had parted, and yet it was not in reality so very long ago. Lady Level remained the best part of the morning, talking of the old days of her happy, yet uneventful, girlhood.

Strolling leisurely through Cavendish Square on her way home, Blanche fell to thinking of the afternoon: speculating where it might be that her husband meant to take her. Perhaps to Hampton Court: she had never seen it, and would like to do so: she would ask him to take her there. Quickening her pace, she soon reached her own door, and saw an empty cab drawn up before it.

"Is any visitor here?" she asked of Sanders, when admitted.

"No, my lady. I have just called the cab for his lordship."

Lord Level came out of the study at the sound of her voice, and turned with her into the front room. She thought he looked vexed—hurried.

"Blanche," he began, "I find I have to run down to Marshdale. But I shall not be away more than a night if I can help it. I shall be back to-morrow if possible; if not, you may expect me the next day for certain."

"To Marshdale!" she repeated, in surprise and vexation. "Then you will not be able to take me out this afternoon! I was hoping it might be to Hampton Court."

"You shall go to Hampton Court when I return."

"Take me with you to Marshdale."

"I cannot," he replied decisively. "I am going down on business."

"Why did you not tell me of it this morning? Why have proposed to———"

"I did not know of it then," he interrupted. "How dismayed you look, Blanche!" he added, half laughing.

"I shall be very lonely, Archibald—all by myself here!"

He said no more, but stooped to kiss her, and left the room, looking at his watch.

"I did not think it was quite so late!" he exclaimed. Turning sharply, for he had been about to enter the study, he approached the front door, hesitated, then turned again, and went into the study.

"No, I can't stop," he said, coming to a final decision, as he once more came forth, shut the study door after him, and locked it, but did not take out the key. "Blanche, don't let anyone come in here; I have left all my papers at sixes and sevens. If I wait to put them up I shall not catch Jenning."

"Are you going to the train now, Archibald?"

"No, no; I want to see Jenning. I shall come back before going to the train."

Getting into the cab, Lord Level was whirled away. Sanders closed the house-door. And Blanche, ascending the stairs to her chamber, in the slow manner we are apt to assume after experiencing some unexpected check, and untying her bonnet as she went up, came upon her maid, Timms. Timms appeared to be in trouble: her face was gloomy and wet with tears.

"What is the matter?" exclaimed her mistress.

"My lady, I can't understand it. My belief is she has *stole* it, and nothing less. But for that dreadful sea-passage, there and back, I'd go over myself to-day, if your ladyship would spare me."

"Now, Timms, what are you talking about?"

"Why, of the box, my lady. I was that vexed at its being left behind that I scribbled a few lines to Victorine from Dover, telling her to get Sauvage not to delay in sending it on. And I've got her answer this morning, denying that any box has been left. Leastways, saying that she can't see it."

While Timms was speaking, she had pulled a note out of her pocket, and offered it to her mistress. It was from their late chambermaid, and written in curious English for Timms' benefit, who was no French scholar, and it certainly denied that the box inquired for, or any other box, had been left behind, so far as she, Victorine, could ascertain.

When departing from Paris three days before, Timms, counting over the luggage with Sanders, discovered at the station that one of the boxes was missing, left behind in their apartments by her own carelessness. The train was on the point of starting, and there was no time to return; but Lord Level despatched a message by a commissionaire to the concierge, Sauvage, to send it on to London by grande vitesse. The box contained wearing apparel belonging to Lady Level, and amidst it a certain dark silk dress which Timms had long coveted. Altogether she was in a state of melancholy self-reproach and had written to Victorine from Dover, urging speed. Victorine's answer, delivered this morning, had completely upset Timms.

Lady Level laughed gaily. "Cheer up, Timms," she said; "the box is on its road. His lordship has had a letter from Madame Sauvage this morning." The concierge himself was no scribe, and his wife always did the writing for him.

Timms dashed her tears away. "Oh, my lady, how thankful I am! What could Victorine mean, I wonder? When was the box sent off? Does your ladyship know?"

"No—o. I—don't know what the letter does say," added Lady Level, calling to mind that she was as yet ignorant of its contents. "I forgot all about it after Lord Level opened it."

Timms did not quite comprehend. "But—I beg your pardon, my lady—I suppose Madame Sauvage does say they have sent it off?"

"I dare say she does. What else should she write for?"

The maid's countenance fell considerably.

"But, my lady," she remonstrated, wise in her superior age and experience, "if—if your ladyship has not read the letter, it may be just the opposite. To pretend, like Victorine, that they have not found the box. Victorine may have spirited it away without their knowledge. She would uncommonly like to get some of those dresses for herself."

This view scarcely appeared feasible to Lady Level. "How silly you are, Timms!" she cried. "You can only look at the dark side of the case. As if Lord Level would not have told me had it been *that* news! I wonder where he put the letter? I will look for it."

"If you would be so kind, my lady! so as to set the doubt at rest."

That she should find the letter on her husband's table, Blanche no more doubted than that it was written by Madame Sauvage to announce the despatch of the box. She ran down to the study, unlocked the door, and entered.

The table was covered with quite a confused mass of papers, heaped one upon another. It seemed as though Lord Level must have been looking for some deed or other. A despatch-box, usually crammed full of papers, stood on the table, open and empty. At the opposite corner was his desk; but that was locked.

For a moment Blanche thought she would abandon her search. The confusion looked too formidable to be meddled with. Well for her own peace of mind that she had not done so!

Bending forward, for papers lay on the carpet as well as the table, she let her eyes range over the litter, slightly lifting with her thumb and forefinger a paper here and there, hoping to discern the required letter. Quite by a stroke of good fortune she came upon it. Good fortune or ill—which?

It lay, together with the two letters which had come with it, under an open parchment, close before Lord Level's chair. One of these letters was from Mr. Jenning, his confidential solicitor, requesting his lordship to be with him at twelve o'clock that morning on a special matter; but that had nothing to do with Blanche, or with us either. She opened the envelope of the one she wished to see, and took out its letter.

But it was not a letter; not, at least, as letters run in general. It was only a piece of thin paper folded once, which bore a few lines in a fine, pointed Italian hand, and in faint-coloured ink, somewhat difficult to decipher.

Now it must be premised that Lady Level had no more thought of prying into what concerned her husband, and did not concern herself, than a child could have had. She would not have been guilty of such a thing for the world. Any one of those parchments or papers, lying open before her eyes, she would have deemed it the height of dishonour to read a word of. This letter from the wife of their late concierge, containing news of her own lost box, was a different matter.

But though the address to Lord Level was undoubtedly in the handwriting of Madame Sauvage, the inside was not. Blanche strained her eyes over it.

> "I arrive to-day at Paris, and find you departed for England with your wife and servants. I come straight on from Pisa, without halting, to inform you of a discovery we have made; there was no time to write. As I am so near, it is well to use the opportunity to pay a short visit to Marshdale to see the child, and I start this evening for it; you can join me there. Pardon the trouble I give you.— NINA."

With her face flaming, with trembling hands, and shortened breath, Lady Level gathered in the words and their meaning. Nina! It was the Italian girl, the base woman who had troubled before her peace of mind, and who must have got Madame Sauvage to address the letter. Evidently she did not mean, the shameless siren, to let Lord Level be at rest. And—and—and what was the meaning of that allusion about "the child"?

Leaving the letter precisely as she had found it, under the sheet of parchment, Lady Level quitted the room and turned the key in the door again. Not for very shame, now that this shameful secret had been revealed to her, would she let her husband know that she had entered. Had she found only what she sought, she would have said openly to him on his return: "Archibald, I went in for Madame Sauvage's note, and I found it. I hope you don't mind—we were anxious about the box." But somehow her eyes were now opened to the fact that she had been guilty of a dishonourable action, one that could not be excused or justified. Had he not locked his door against intruders—herself as well as others?

Passing into the front room, where the table was now being laid for luncheon, which they took at one o'clock, she drew a chair near the fire, mechanically watching Sanders as he placed the dishes on the table, in reality seeing nothing; her mind was in a tumult, very painful and rebellious.

Timms came stealing in. How any lady could be so indifferent as her lady when a box of beautiful clothes was at stake, Timms could not understand: sitting quietly there over the fire, and never coming back to set a body's mind at rest with yes or no.

"I beg pardon for intruding," began Timms, with deprecation, "but did your ladyship find Madame Sauvage's letter?"

"No," curtly replied Lady Level. "I dare say the box is lost. Not much matter if it is."

Timms withdrew, lifting her hands in condemning displeasure when she got outside. "Not much matter! if ever I heard the like of that! A whole trunk *full!* and some of 'em *lovely!*"

"Will you sit down, now, my lady, or wait for his lordship?" inquired Sanders.

Lady Level answered the question by taking her place at table. She felt as though she should never care to wait for his lordship again, for luncheon or anything else. In a few minutes a cab dashed up to the door, bringing him.

"That's right, Blanche; I am glad you did not wait for me," he began. "Sanders, is my hand-bag ready?"

"Quite, my lord."

"Put it into the cab, then."

He hastened into the study as he spoke, and began putting things straight there with a deft and rapid hand. In an incredibly short time, the papers were all in order, locked up in their various receptacles, and the table was cleared.

"Good-bye, my love," said he, returning to the front room.

"Do you not take anything to eat?" asked Blanche, in short and sullen tones, which he was in too great a hurry to notice.

"No: or I should lose the train."

He caught her to him. Blanche turned her face away.

"You silly child! you are cross with me for leaving you. My dear, believe me, *I could not help it.* Charley is coming up to dine with you this evening."

Leaving his kisses on her lips, but getting none in return, Lord Level went out to the cab. As it drove away, there came up to the door a railway luggage van. The lost box had arrived from Paris. Timms knelt down with extra fervour that night to offer up her thanksgivings.

Lord Level had snatched a moment to look in upon me, and ask me to dine with Blanche that evening.

"She is not pleased at being left alone," he said; "but I am obliged to run down to Marshdale. And, Charley, she saw something about Tom in the paper this morning: I had to turn it off in the best way I could: so be cautious if she mentions it to you."

I had meant to look again after Tom Heriot that evening, but could not refuse this. Blanche was unusually silent throughout dinner.

"Is anything the matter, Blanche?" I asked her, when we were in the drawing-room.

"A great deal is the matter," she replied resentfully. "I am not going to put up with it."

"Put up with what?"

"Oh—with Lord Level. With his—his deceit. But I can't tell you now, Charles: I shall speak to himself first."

I laughed. "More jealousy cropping up! What has he done now, Blanche?"

"What has he gone to Marshdale for?" retorted Blanche, her cheeks flaming. "And what did he go to Pisa for when we were last in Paris?" continued she, without any pause. "He *did* go. It was in December; and he was away ten days."

"Well,' I suppose some matter or other called him there," I said. "As to Marshdale—it is his place; his home. Why should this annoy you, Blanche? A man cannot carry his wife with him everywhere."

"*I* know," she said, catching up her fan, and beginning to use it sharply. "I know more than you do, Charles. More than he thinks for—a great deal more."

"It strikes me, my dear, that you are doing your best to estrange your husband from you—if you speak to him as you are speaking now. That will not enhance your own happiness, Blanche."

"The fault is his," she cried, turning her hot face defiantly upon me.

"It may be. I don't think so."

"He does not care for me *at all*. He cares for—for—somebody else."

"You may be mistaken. I should be sorry to believe it. But, even should it be so—listen, Blanche—even should it be so, you will do well to change your tactics. *Try and win him back to you.* I tell it you for the sake of your own happiness."

Blanche tossed back her golden curls, and rose. "How old-fashioned you are, Charles! it is of no use talking to you. Will you sing our old duet with me—'I've wandered in dreams'?"

"Ay. But I am out of practice."

She had taken her place on the music-stool, and was playing the first bars of the song, when a thought struck her, and she turned round.

"Charley, such a curious thing happened this morning. I saw in the *Times* a list of some escaped convicts, who had been on their way to Van Diemen's Land, and amongst them was the name of Thomas Heriot. For a moment it startled and frightened me."

Her eyes were upon my face, so was the light. Having a piece of music in my hand, I let it fall, and stooped to pick it up.

"Was it not strange, Charles?"

"Not particularly so. There may be a hundred Tom Heriots in the world."

"That's what Archibald said—or something to the same effect. But, do you know, I cannot get it out of my head. And Tom's not writing to us from India has seemed to me all day more strangely odd than it did before."

"India is a regular lazy place. The heat makes people indolent and indifferent."

"Yes, I know. Besides, as papa said to me in the few minutes we were talking together before he went away, Tom may have written, and the letters not have reached us. The mail from India is by no means a safe one, he says; letters often get lost by it."

"By no means safe: no end of letters are lost continually," I murmured, seconding old Carlen's invention, knowing not what else to say. "Let us go on, Blanche. It is I who begin, I think—'I've wandered in dreams.'"

Wandered in dreams! If this misery connected with Tom Heriot were only a dream, and not a reality!

END OF VOL. II.

9 789362 923288